all that Glitters

Josée Chouinard

with Lynda D. Prouse

Foreword by Kurt Browning

Fenn Publishing Company Ltd.
Bolton, Canada

ALL THAT GLITTERS

A Fenn Publishing Book / February 2002

Fenn Publishing Company Ltd.
Bolton, Canada

National Library of Canada Cataloguing in Publication Data

Chouinard, Josée, 1969–
All That Glitters

ISBN 1-55168-260-5

1. Chouinard, Josée, 1969– 2. Skating. I. Prouse, Lynda. II. Title

GV850.C45A3 2002   796.91'2'092   C2001-903770-8

Printed and Bound in Canada

*To my dad. The fighter in you is alive
in me today. And to my mom for your loving
devotion to Eric and me.*

— Josée Chouinard

*To my husband David Szabo.
Your patience, love, and support are immeasurable. I have no better friend than you.*

— Lynda D. Prouse

ACKNOWLEDGMENTS

Thank you to: my husband, Jean-Michel Bombardier, who gave me the confidence a woman needs. I am so glad you found me – or did I find you? Lynda Prouse, for your perserverance and patience in making this book a reality. It has been a wonderful experience working with you. My brother, Eric, who became the man in my family at such an early age. All of my friends who keep my life balanced, including Isabelle, Lloyd, Kurt, Brian, Chantal, Martin, and Maggie. Special thanks to my friend and agent, Nathalie Cook; my skating club, Les Lames d'Argent; the Quebec Skating Federation; my coach Joanne Barbeau; and Lucien Roy. And to everyone else who has made a difference in my life, my love and thanks.

Josée Chouinard

Thank you to: my mother Vera Prouse and my sister Marlene Dick for your unconditional love and understanding; Arnold Gosewich for being the agent I expected and more; Jordan Fenn for believing in this project as much as I did; and Michael Rosenberg for your encouragement. Thanks also to Lisa Herdman, Lloyd Eisler, Isabelle Brasseur, and Jozef Sabovcik.

Lynda D. Prouse

Other Books by Lynda D. Prouse

BRASSEUR & EISLER — To Catch a Dream

JOZEF SABOVCIK — Jumpin' Joe:
The Jozef Sabovcik Story

ELIZABETH MANLEY — As I Am:
My Life After the Olympics

BRASSEUR & EISLER — The Professional Years

CONTENTS

To know Josée is to love her. If you're lucky enough to meet her, you will immediately notice her delightful voice, amazing smile, sparkling eyes, and contagious energy. And, of course, her wonderful laugh. You see, Josée is the full package deal. Each and every one of her characteristics compliments the next. A pure source of goodwill, sweetness, and honesty, it's no wonder she is one of my favourite people.

And the lady knows how to skate. Simply put, if there was a category for the best of the least-decorated women skaters, Josée would win. In fact, I've seen her win both the World Championships and the Olympics while practicing with me. Her talent as a competitor never got to reach its potential, but her talent as a skater did. Technically superb and always creative, Josée knows how to draw an audience in with her expressive skating style. She's a natural at this sport but she also worked hard to get where she is.

And even though Josée went through some difficult times, she kept her sense of humour and optimism. I have seen her extremely sad now and then, but there was always a smile behind the tears. I can remember the two of us walking and talking once, and Josée commented that she had some really tough times at some very big public moments in her life . . . and then she burst into a fit of laughter. That's Josée. She got down sometimes, but she never gave up on herself.

Read on and get a look at the world of figure skating through Josée's eyes. I'm certain you'll enjoy her viewpoints and will learn more about our sport along the way. And as you flip through these pages, it won't take you long to find out why I'm so proud to call her my friend.

It's true!

Kurt Browning

INTRODUCTION

Although I had seen Josée skate at many events, we were first introduced in 1996. She had been going through a difficult time with her career, and the emotional upset showed on her face. It's not easy for this personable skater to hide her feelings. Wanting to offer some words of encouragement, I told Josée that she was one of my father's favourite figure skaters. "Oh," she said, as the tears welled up in her eyes, "I wish he was here now to tell me himself. I would have loved to have talked to him."

Josée won my heart over from that moment on. You see, when I later told my dad what Josée had said, it made his day. Not long after, he was taken ill and has since passed away. While doing our interviews, Josée and I often thought that both our beloved fathers were "up there" directing the course of this book. Her own father had influenced her greatly with her skating, as mine did with my writing.

When I approached Josée about collaborating on a book, I had wanted to work with her on an autobiography. I knew she had a story to tell. But Josée was hesitant, uncertain as to whether she was ready. So we decided to put together something different. Based on her own experiences, this book is part biographical, part educational, and part motivational. It will be particularly beneficial to skaters at all levels, but will also appeal to figure skating fans and anyone else who appreciates an honest first-person account of heartbreak, hardship, and ultimate triumph.

Working with Josée was so much fun, and I hope you get as much pleasure reading this book as I did writing it.

Lynda D. Prouse

CHAPTER ONE

Talk About Pressure!

Just imagine. The event I was about to compete in was being watched by millions of people worldwide. In fact, I later learned that it was one of the highest-viewed television shows in history, thanks to the drama surrounding Nancy Kerrigan and Tonya Harding. But at the time, I was blissfully unaware that so many were tuned in. Lucky for me, because I don't think I could have handled the extra pressure.

It was day twelve of the 1994 Winter Olympics. Staged in Lillehammer, Norway, the Games were supposed to be the pinnacle of my amateur career. I had worked long hours to be there and had made tremendous changes in my life, all for the sport I loved so much. Now, if I skated to my potential, an Olympic medal would be well within my grasp.

I had been skating perfectly in practice for the past two weeks. My coach and I felt good about this because a few days before I left for Norway, I could hardly walk, let alone skate. While training, I developed severe and painful muscle spasms in my back. Since injuring it in a series of falls when I was a teenager, my back tended to give me trouble if I was under stress or training too much. But after intensive massage therapy, I was on my feet and skating in peak form. Actually, I had been skating well all season, coming second behind Nancy Kerrigan at Pirouetten, a major international event that was held at the Olympic arena. From there I went on to win my third national title at the Canadian Championships in January.

Knowing that this would be my last Olympics, I had decided to enjoy the entire experience from start to finish, and that meant arriving early to participate in the opening ceremony with the rest of the Canadian team. Two years earlier at the 1992 Games, where I placed ninth, I was in Albertville only long enough to compete, and regretted missing out on so much. Although skating and training was my obvious focus, this time I planned to see as much as I could of the Olympics and support my friends throughout their own competitions.

Two days before my event, I was in the stands to see Kurt Browning's magical performance of "Casablanca." He and I had trained together all season under well-known coach Louis Stong. More important, we had become close friends. I was so sad for Kurt when he had problems with his technical program, because I knew how hard he had worked for this moment. But he redeemed himself with the free skate, and although he didn't win a medal, Kurt certainly won the hearts of the audience. Elvis Stojko, another friend of mine, won the silver, and I was very proud of him. And of course, no one cheered louder than I did when Isabelle Brasseur and Lloyd Eisler took a bronze medal in pairs. Isabelle and I were roommates at the Olympic Village, as we usually were whenever we competed at international events. She and I were almost like sisters and respected each other immensely.

On the day of the ladies short program, tickets were being sold outside the Northern Lights Hall arena for $2,000, which was 10 times their worth. It was no secret that everyone wanted to see Tonya and Nancy skate. Ever since Nancy had been clubbed on the knee a month earlier at the United States National Championships, women's figure skating had come under a glaring global spotlight, and the Olympics had become a media circus. And while probably neither one of them wanted it, centre stage belonged to the two U.S. skaters.

It was all very strange. During the weeks before my competition, I would arrive at the rink for practice and no one from the media would be there. But if Nancy or Tonya was scheduled to practice after me, the arena would fill with reporters and television cameras, and the quiet rink would be transformed into a noisy zoo. If they happened to practice before my group, the arena would be packed when we arrived, but would empty out as soon as the women left the building. Before the long program, I was on the same practice ice as Tonya, and the cameras wouldn't stop flashing until she quit skating. She decided to leave halfway through the practice, and the media horde followed her out the door. I found it quite disturbing.

Because there was so much interest in these two skaters before and during the Olympics, I didn't find myself as nervous as I normally was at a major competition. Usually, I can't sleep and by the time the event takes place, I almost feel as if I am going to die. I just want it to happen so badly. When the competition finally arrives, my adrenalin is running very high and it carries me through the program. I'm nervous, but in a positive way. Ever since I was a little girl and first began to compete, I have visualized those nervous feelings as little bugs fluttering around inside me. When I am mentally prepared and strongly focused on a competition, I picture the bugs getting into a perfect line and allowing me to skate at my highest level.

At this event, no one was paying attention to me or most of the other skaters. Coupled with the knowledge that I had been skating extremely well in practice, I had allowed myself to become very relaxed. I was excited, but I didn't have the extra nervousness I required to focus. Don't get me wrong. I certainly wasn't the picture of calm. After all, this was the Olympics and I wouldn't be myself if I didn't allow some nerves to creep in. No matter what the situation is, I tend to put too much pressure on myself, and this time was no different.

Before the technical program began, I was probably at my worst when I was still back at my room in the Olympic Village applying my makeup. Ladies' figure skating is a demanding sport that requires a great deal of athletic talent, but it is also an image sport. The way we look on the ice is as important as how we perform. Cosmetics, costumes, and perfectly coiffed hairstyles all contribute to the glamorous image. They are also what make us different from other Olympic athletes, who would often tease us, saying they knew when a female figure skater was approaching by the scent of perfume and hairspray.

But aside from the fact that I must look good on the ice, applying my makeup before a competition is when the game actually begins for me. As I put on my eyeshadow, mascara, and lipstick, everything about the upcoming event is running through my mind at a mile a minute. Although I do my best to try and think only positive thoughts, little negative voices will sneak in and it can sometimes result in a major fight between the two sides. I also have a superstition. I have found that if my makeup looks great, I don't seem to skate as well as I do when my makeup goes wrong. On the day of my technical program, my makeup had never looked better. Shades of things to come, I guess.

The bus ride over to the arena was long, so I slipped on my Discman and listened to some of my favourite music, all the while imagining my-self on the ice. Visualization and imagery are very important in figure skating, or any sport for that matter. This is where you see yourself in your mind performing in front of an audience and judges. I also imagine how I am going to feel during that performance. During the bus ride, I pictured myself skating a perfect program. Ear-lier, during my practice sessions, I had walked all around the rink, examining each corner. I make a habit of doing this before every major competi-tion, to become familiar with the angles. Then I can envision what it will look and feel like when I am the only one on the ice going into a combi-nation jump, skating backwards, or getting ready for my triple Lutz. I'll know exactly where I will be, and so when it comes time to actually per-form my routine, every step and element will be like déjà vu.

As with any World Championship or Olympic event I'd participated in, my schedule was de-tailed to the moment. But wherever I am com-peting, I prefer to get to the rink early and social-ize a little. People stop and talk to you, and you have to make time for that. After saying my hel-los at the Olympic arena, I tried to block every-thing else out. Before an event of this magnitude, the competitors tend to act like horses with blind-ers on. Still in my warm-up suit, I jogged around the rink and I remember seeing Nancy Kerrigan running as well. We all have different ways of preparing ourselves for the competition. Some of the skaters may be walking through their pro-grams, while others are stretching. Many are lis-tening to music, visualizing their performances, and others are in quiet conference with their coaches. We usually keep our distance from each other.

After I finished my run, I went to the dressing room and slipped into my costume. It was a peri-winkle blue dress in a Juliette style that seemed to float around me. The shoulders were trimmed with lifelike flowers and when Sébastien Britten, a friend of mine and one of the skaters on the Canadian team, saw the dress, he joked that it looked as if I was carrying my garden around with me. But it was so pretty and beautifully suited for "La Fille Mal Gardé," the program I was about to perform. Funny, but when Mary Jane Stong, my coach's wife and partner, had first brought me the music, I had no interest in skating to it. But the first time I moved on the ice to the haunt-ing melody, I felt like it was made for me. Sandra Bezic then choreographed the piece, as she did my long program, "An American in Paris." Hav-ing skated both programs hundreds of times, by this point I could have probably performed them in my sleep.

Waiting by the boards to get on the ice for the six-minute warm-up, I glanced up at the large crowd in the arena. Supporters of the skaters from various countries were clearly visible in the stands. Many waved flags and all appeared to be in high spirits. I knew my mother and my boyfriend, Jean-Michel Bombardier, were in the crowd. At least I hoped they were. My mother, in particular, has a very poor sense of direction. When I was a child she was forever getting lost at shopping malls, and more recently, she and Jean-Michel's mother couldn't find their way out of a hotel parking lot! They drove around in circles for ages, laughing the whole time, but still hopelessly lost.

These Games covered a vast area, and since I wasn't able to see my mother before the event, I wondered if she had found her way to the correct venue. It's difficult to see anyone at the Olympics because security is so tight, and friends and relations aren't allowed backstage before the competition unless they are also professionally associated with the skater (for example, Surya Bonaly's mother is also her coach). Even visiting the athletes at the Village is strictly regimented. And at this Olympics, the ladies figure skating competition was particularly well-guarded because of the hoopla surrounding Tonya and Nancy. But even if security hadn't been so stringent, my mother would never come backstage before a major event. She wouldn't want to be anywhere near me because she is far more nervous than I am, and wouldn't know what to say to me. On the other hand, Jean-Michel, who is now my husband, is very familiar with the world of competitive figure skating. Although he didn't make the Olympic team that year, he would go on to become Canadian pairs champion with his partner at the time, Michelle Menzies.

I was getting anxious to begin, and as soon as the door opened, I stepped on the ice along with the rest of the ladies in my group for the warm-up. Many people believe that during this pre-performance skate, the competitors are playing mind games as they eye one another. However, for most of us, it is just our way of focusing. We are not only examining each other, but also everything else around us. Speaking only for myself, I am attempting to make the environment my own as I get comfortable on the ice. I suppose some skaters try to unnerve a competitor, but I have never played those kinds of games, believing them to be a waste of valuable time. On this night, my body was a little stiff, so I warmed up more than usual and when we were called off the ice, I felt good.

It was at the start of my program, while waiting for my music to begin, that the enormity of the event suddenly flashed in my mind. The climax of my amateur skating career was about to unfold, and I realized that my future and everything I had worked for depended on how well I did. I found myself on the ice thinking, This is it. I am facing the end of my career and now I have $2^1/2$ minutes to prove myself. I only wish I would have dealt with this reality beforehand, but I didn't. Those little bugs were all over the place when I began my routine and I just couldn't control them.

Preparing for a double-toe combination, I skated by the boards, and as I was about to take off, I happened to catch sight of my coach. For that one fraction of a second, I lost my already shaky focus and didn't complete the combination. In total shock, I looked over to Louis in confusion. I hadn't missed that jump in almost three weeks of practice! The look on my coach's face clearly reflected his own bewilderment. But there was no time for analyzing. It wasn't the first time I had missed a jump in a program and wouldn't be the last time. You learn to move on. I endeavoured to pay more attention to the music and concentrate on each step and movement. But I was now on automatic pilot, still stunned from my mistake, and it was difficult to skate with any enthusiasm. My face is very transparent of my feelings, whether I am on the ice or off, and the emotional aspects of the program failed to shine through.

Sitting in the "kiss-and-cry" area with Louis after my performance, I was disappointed and filled with a terrible sense of shame. Feeling this way was unfamiliar to me because I had always skated for myself in the past. But now I had an overwhelming certainty that I had let Canada down. When you represent your country at an event of this magnitude and prestige, you know that people back home are watching and pinning their hopes on you. I was so upset that I couldn't look anyone in the eye. All my dreams had just about vanished in a brief $2^1/2$ minutes. There was no going back. I couldn't do it again. In that short time, everything had fallen apart and I just wanted to escape to the solitude of my room.

We had a day between the short and long programs, and at practice, I practically flew through
my jumps. However, I remember thinking, "Even
though I'm skating well, it really doesn't matter
now. It was yesterday that I wasn't supposed to
miss a jump." Since I had come eighth in the
short, I figured that the podium was likely out of
reach, and that even if I had an amazing performance, if everyone else skated up to par, the best
I could probably do was fourth. Leaving for the
rink, I was sadder than I had been in a long time,
believing that all the physical and mental training I had endured had been for nothing.

Because I was feeling so down, I thought I
should go to the arena earlier than usual. Maybe
if I was at the rink, I thought, I would be able to
get into the mood to compete. The adrenalin and
nerves just weren't there, however. I have to be
happy to skate well, and I couldn't find any measure of happiness in my being. Louis attempted
to lift my spirits and put a smile on my face, but
nothing he said could make me feel better. Wanting to be alone for awhile, I decided to step outside and get a breath of fresh air.

While I was standing behind the arena, I noticed a bus pull up. When the doors opened, most
of the women I would be competing against
stepped off the vehicle. One by one, Nancy
Kerrigan, Yuka Sato, Katarina Witt, and the others filed into the rink. They were all ahead of me
in the standings, and it bothered me because I
knew I was just as good as they were. Still feeling

11

a little sorry for myself, I was abruptly struck by the thought that if I performed up to my ability, I could come close to the top in the free skate. I may not win a medal, I thought, but at least I would be satisfied with the knowledge that I had done my best. Normally, I don't worry about trying to beat my competitors. I only go up against myself and how well I skated at my last performance. But at that point, I believed that my whole career had fallen apart and I had failed to achieve my ultimate goal. For me, this was using drastic measures, but I soon felt the adrenalin kick in, and it lit the fire to fight. As an icy wind hit my face, I smiled. I had been so lost in thought that I was unaware of the freezing cold weather. I quickly went inside to begin my warm-up routine, feeling more determined than I had in a long time.

After the skating warm-up, I came off the ice and went down a hallway to sit quietly by myself. I put headphones over my ears and listened to music while I visualized my program. My coach was perhaps 10 feet away from me and, every now and then, I glanced at the television monitors that were scattered around backstage to see how long I had before it was my turn to perform. By the luck of the draw, Tonya was skating before me. I heard later that some people wondered if it bothered me to follow her, but to tell you the truth, she was the least of my worries. Tonya seemed to be very unhappy, and because a good attitude plays such an important role in how we skate, I knew she wouldn't be at her best.

I had already gone through the program in my head when I looked over at the monitor. Although I couldn't hear what was going on, I noticed that Tonya was standing by the judging panel, and I assumed that something had gone wrong with her program. The rules have since changed, but back then a skater could appeal to the judges, who may allow the skater to start his or her program over or perform it again later on. At the time, I didn't realize that Tonya's lace had broken, but I could see she was upset. Presuming the judges would let her fix whatever was wrong and start her program over, I believed I would have at least 4^1/$_2$ minutes before I had to be on the ice. Usually, when the skater before me is about halfway finished, I get up and move closer to the door that opens to the ice. This allows my eyes to become accustomed to the bright television lights while I get the feel of the audience. But believing that Tonya would be starting over, I thought I had plenty of time. So I stayed seated and began to run through my program again.

Sitting quietly before I compete is especially important to me. If I were to stand around while I wait, I would become so jittery that I'd probably be jumping all over the place. To skate well, I must be calm. Otherwise, with my high energy level and the rush of adrenalin I get when I step on the ice to perform, I would move so fast that I could skate a four-minute program in two minutes. So I must bring my mind into a restful place, where I am happy and at peace with myself. Ideally, my breathing will slow down to a point where I am almost asleep. Then I try and get a handle on those little bugs inside me. If I don't, they will be flying everywhere and I will have no control whatsoever. So I have to sit down and line them up inside of me. Everything has to settle into its place. I strive to relax my body and remove any tension or weight from my shoulders. I let it all drop around to my feet.

Just as I was in the midst of my mental preparation, I noticed my coach waving at me. Taking the headphones off my ears, I heard one of the team leaders complaining to my coach, "They can't do that!" I had no idea what he was referring to. Then I saw that Louis was giving me the sign to come forward, and it dawned on me that I was supposed to get on the ice. As I was soon to discover, the judges had decided to give Tonya time to fix her lace, and meanwhile they wanted me to perform my program ahead of schedule.

In a panic, I began to run, but my coach loudly yelled at me to walk. I followed his orders, but let me tell you that I could have won a marathon, I was walking so fast. My heart was beating furiously and in a few seconds, I went from being extremely calm to a complete nervous wreck. Too bad I didn't have a camera inside me filming all those little bugs. They were flying up, down, and all around. It was like they were having a party in my stomach, but had forgotten to invite me. All my mental preparation was for nothing.

As I stood at the boards removing my skate guards, I shook with anxiety. Then the crowd began to clap. They started slowly, then faster and faster. I think they were trying to say, "We're behind you, Josée." The applauding was soon replaced by loud cheers as my name was announced. It seemed as if the audience's emotions were running as high as mine. I knew they were rooting for me, but because I had lost my focus on the way to the ice, I found the noise very distracting.

I started my program, went into the triple flip, and crashed on the ice. Then I rushed into my second jump and put my hand down. I was going so fast that Jean-Michel told me later that it looked like I had an engine pushing me. After my second mishap, I realized that I couldn't go any faster than my music and forced myself to slow down. From there, I skated as best I could. I executed a triple toe and a triple loop. The latter jump was easy for me in practice, but often gave me difficulty in competition.

If there is one thing that I am proud of from that performance, it was that I didn't give up, which would have been easy to do. Even under those difficult circumstances, I tried my hardest and did my best. Still, when I was finished, I skated off the ice feeling very upset with myself, believing I should have handled what happened before I got on the ice better.

Afterwards, people commented that the judges should have given me more time to prepare. They also remarked that Tonya shouldn't have been allowed to redo her program later on. Everyone wanted to blame someone other than me. I do believe that Tonya got a break from the judges. She had already missed a jump when her lace broke, but they gave her a second chance. If she was skating in today's competitive world, and the same thing happened, she would have had to fix her problem and get back on the ice within two minutes. Then she would have had to begin her program from wherever she had stopped.

Having said that, however, I put the blame for my situation squarely on myself. I certainly had enough experience to know that the judges would have waited for me. I should have finished my mental preparation and brought that sense of calm onto the ice with me. I had the control, but I didn't take it. When I was called early, I rushed out and did what I was told. In those days, I would never have dreamed of questioning my coach, a judge, or a decision that was made. It just wasn't in my personality to make a fuss. I was a people pleaser and wanted everyone's approval.

Some time later, when I was going through a depressing period, trying to figure out my career and life, I rediscovered something I had been taught as a teenager but had not fully utilized during the later stages of my amateur career. We each have the power to control our environment to some extent. The night I skated my long program at the Olympics, I put so much pressure on myself to succeed that instead of taking charge, I allowed the environment to control me. But I know now there will always be pressures in life, whether they come from competitive sports, school, career, or relationships. There will be decisions and choices to make about how we want to live our lives. It is how we deal with pressure or rejection that is important. It used to hurt me if I thought anyone was angry with me – and if someone didn't like me, I would be devastated. Over the years, I have worked on this, and although I still try to please people, I have learned that I must come first. If I am happy, then I will make other people happy. I have also come to realize that the only person you can totally satisfy is yourself. Trying to gain everyone else's approval is an incredible waste of energy. It just won't happen.

Nancy Kerrigan placed second at those Olympics behind Oksana Baiul. Tonya Harding skated her program again and placed eighth. I was ninth. My friends tried to console me afterwards by saying that at least I was in the top 10. But for me it was the second time I had come ninth at the Olympics. I hated that position. My expectations were so much higher.

Later, I attended a party with the rest of the athletes at Canada House. Most of them were in a jovial mood, celebrating medals, sharing memories, and generally glad the pressures of the Games were almost over. I tried to get into the spirit of the party, but my eyes kept misting over. I couldn't stop thinking about what had happened. Taking me by the hand, Jean-Michel led me outside, then suggested we go for a walk. Crunching through the snow together, I began to weep with frustration. He said, "Oh, you are not going to cry. At least you made it to the Olympics. I wish I had."

In 1992, Jean-Michel had missed making the Olympic team and it was very painful for him. While I went to Albertville to compete, he took off on a vacation. In a sense, he was running away. When he and Michelle didn't make the 1994 team, he was again heartbroken. But this time, he decided to live the Olympic experience anyway. He had dreamt of going to the Olympics and he would go! With very little money, Jean-Michel arrived in Paris with only a backpack. From there he took a train to Norway, and somehow found a room.

He was quite an inspiration to me, and although I didn't want to hear it at the time, eventually I realized how lucky I was to have made it that far. We walked a little further and came upon a type of sled that is commonly used by the Norwegians to get around on their everyday business. Jean-Michel picked me up, put me in the sled, and together we went flying down one of the many hills at a breathtaking speed. It was exhilarating! And for the first time since my competition, I laughed out loud in sheer delight.

But later, and for a long time afterwards, I couldn't shake the feelings of anguish that resulted from failing to realize my dream. I also believed that I had let my country down in such a way that I didn't know if I could keep going and try again in 1998. I had trained so long for this moment. How could I do it all again? Skating had been my life since I was eight years old. Over the years it had built my character and enhanced my personality, but over the next several months it would come close to destroying me.

As I sat under the clear Norwegian skies the following night, watching the closing ceremonies, I pulled my coat closer around me and tried to enjoy the pageantry. But my mind was elsewhere. In it I could see a little girl with long hair hanging in her eyes. She was laughing as she glided across the ice, imagining she was a flying bird. It was a glorious feeling of freedom and fun. I was that little girl, and now I longed to go back to those simpler times, when my life didn't revolve around gold medals and disappointment. Then, I had embraced the sport with a pure and abiding joy. I couldn't wait for my parents to take me to the rink, so I could slide and spin and jump. It was a time of laughter and excitement. Skating had been my passion for most of my life. And now, I truly believed that it had all come to an end.

CHAPTER TWO

Go Figure

Look at a picture of me when I was eight years old and you'd never guess that I was a figure skater. With baby fat around my middle and a decided preference for jeans over dresses, I wasn't much like the other girls at the rink. And although I loved skating from the moment I first stepped on the ice, I was just as happy playing soccer or baseball with the neighbourhood boys.

Born in Rosemont, Quebec on August 21, 1969, my life was all about sports and competition from a very early age. I just couldn't seem to stop moving, and that is probably why I favoured the company of boys over girls. Even though I studied and did my homework with girlfriends, most of them were just too slow for me when it came to outdoor activities. And besides, they spent too much time worrying about their clothes and hair. No frilly dresses that had to be kept clean for me! I was forever coming home dirty, but proud that I had again been one of the first chosen for the after-school ball team.

One of the games that I looked forward to was balon chasseur (hunter ball). Played on a drawn-out rectangular court, we took a large ball and threw it at opposing team members. If the ball was caught, the person was still alive. If the person dropped it, he or she was dead and had to leave the game. The team with the most remaining players won the game. I loved winning balon chasseur. But I liked to win at everything. Walking to school with a girlfriend, I would unexpectedly bolt ahead of her and shout, "Beat you!" She would look at me as if I was crazy, because I hadn't bothered to tell her that we were in a race. Even my schoolwork had to be the best. If I was doing a presentation in class, I wanted it to be better than everyone else's and would be quite perturbed if another student outdid me. I looked upon anything challenging as fun.

I think I came by my ambitious personality quite naturally. My dad was an amateur boxer before he and my mother married, and there was no one more ready for a challenge than he. One summer we visited my mom's family, who owned a horse farm. My uncles and my father went out for a ride and were on their way back when the horses sensed they were near the stable. As he was an inexperienced rider, my dad didn't realize that the closer a horse gets to the barn, the faster the animal will go in anticipation of food, water, and a rest. Because my dad wanted to arrive ahead of the others, he spurred his horse into a gallop. As they neared the barn, my father was unable to stop. The horse reared back, threw him, and he landed inches away from a large metal farm implement. Although my father was bruised and cut, he wasn't seriously hurt. But he could have killed himself trying to be number one. I was frightened for him that day, yet I understood why he wanted to be ahead of the others.

With dark hair, green almond-shaped eyes, and a dimple in his chin like me, my father, André, is the subject of my first memory. I couldn't have been more than three years old, but the image is so clear in my mind. We were in a store at an Indian reservation in Quebec when I spotted a tiny Eskimo doll. As I touched the soft fur of the parka that surrounded her face, I wished out loud that I could have such a doll. My dad must have seen or heard me, but he didn't say anything. When we left the store, he pulled the doll out of a bag and gave it to me. I was so excited and surprised by this special gift.

He and my mother, Raymonde, were opposites in many ways. She was petite, and although she is darker now, she had golden hair in those days. Shy and protective of me and my younger brother, Eric, she usually went along with whatever my dad decided, and he tended to be more easygoing about our upbringing. He was also the one who handled the household finances, as was typical of that era. I can recall what happened when my brother and I needed clothes at the start of a new school year. Dad gave Mom a credit card and told her to take us out and buy whatever was required.

Having no idea what was in the bank account or how much she could afford to spend, my mother cautiously selected two outfits for each of us. When we got home, she showed my father our purchases. He said, "They go to school for more than two days a week," and insisted we return to the store the next day to buy more outfits. I was ecstatic, because even at that young age, I loved to shop.

I simply adored my father, and when he passed away when I was 12, I was devastated. While he was alive, I was as outgoing and bold as he was. My mother tells me that as a toddler, I would sit at the curb in front of our house and say hello to anyone who walked by on the street. Apparently nothing delighted me more than if the stranger would stop and carry on a conversation. Mom says that I wasn't naughty or loud, but had a way of drawing attention to myself whenever I wanted. I just found it easy to talk and relate to people of any age. But after my father died, something changed inside of me and I became timid and insecure.

Dad was an engineer for Air Canada, while my mom worked in the admissions department of a hospital in Montreal, where she is still employed today. They were both busy with their jobs and children, but always found time to ski on the weekends, a sport they both enjoyed. Of course, that was before I started to skate.

When I was seven years old, my next-door neighbour, Natalie, told me how much fun she was having at the skating rink. Wanting to see for myself, I asked my parents to buy me a pair of skates. They agreed but had no idea of what they were getting into. Taking a Saturday off from skiing, we headed to the rink instead, where I had a great time playing on the ice with my friends. I don't think I would have been considered a natural talent the first time I skated. I mean, I didn't immediately leap into a double Axel or anything. However, I also didn't fall down too much. (Then again, I probably walked more than I skated.) I do remember how much fun it was though, and before long I was skating on Saturday mornings in group lessons at the larger of the two clubs in Laval, the city we had moved to a month after I was born.

There were approximately 2,500 skaters at this rink, and at least 21 of them were assigned to each amateur coach. These coaches answered to one professional coach, who was also the director of the rink. There was very little space to move around in. It was so crowded with other students that sometimes it would take up to three weeks before I would get any personal attention from my teacher. After a year, I had earned two badges towards the regulatory Canadian Figure Skating Association (CFSA) program, which my dad thought was extraordinary. Since it took 14 badges to finish before moving on to the next level, he believed I would be an Olympian within seven years. Looking back now, it seems quite funny, because if a child took private lessons, he or she could easily earn eight badges in one year. But my dad was like, Oh my God, we have one hell of a talent here!

I idolized my first coach. Her name was Diane Telchat and she taught me the basic jumps. First I learned the waltz and Salchow (named after Ulrich Salchow of Sweden). At that level, neither jump required much talent from the young skater because they were half-jumps. Then I learned the loop and flip, which were more difficult to grasp because they were full rotations. The Lutz (named after Tomas Lutz of Italy) and Axel (named after Axel Paulsen of Norway) would come later. One day, about a year after I started skating, we noticed an announcement hanging on the wall of our club. It was a call for entries to a competition in a small town outside of Montreal. Diane asked my dad if he wanted me to enter, and he immediately agreed. My coach and I made up a little solo number that I practiced for a few weeks before the competition. Meanwhile, my mother was busy making a costume. She finished it a day before the competition, and I thought it was the most beautiful dress in the world. Bright yellow, with navy piping running down the middle, it was cut out of a velvet material that stretched only on one side (unthinkable for today's competitive costumes, where stretch is all too important). But in the mid-seventies, it was considered to be an innovative fabric compared to the rigid and bulky materials of days gone by.

It was at this competition that I became totally hooked on skating. My coach and I were in the dressing room, where she was applying makeup to my face. It seemed as if there were so many important people bustling around, but when I think back now, most of them were probably just the parents and coaches of the skaters. It was all so exciting and different from my everyday practices at the club sessions, where my skating outfit had graduated from pants to a pale blue skating skirt, beige tights, white sweater, and matching turtleneck. Everyone was fussing around the other girls, who I loved looking at. Many of them were older and some wore colourful, sparkling dresses. I was fascinated by the glamour of it all. And then there was the smell. It wasn't like your ordinary dressing room, which at times can be quite unpleasant. Every corner of this room was filled with the scent of hairspray. It was all so feminine – a far cry from kicking the soccer ball around with the boys.

My coach explained that I would be allowed to skate a three or four-minute warm-up, and pointed out the stand that had been erected for the judges. Previously, I had no concept of what a competition was and still didn't fully understand the role of the judges. While on the ice with the other skaters for the warm-up, I noticed the way they performed the flip and loop jumps. Up until then, I had been cheating on mine by finishing half of the rotation on the ice. Now it clicked, and I couldn't wait to include the jumps in my program, executing them the way they were supposed to be done. Before I knew it, I was being called onto the ice to perform in front of an audience for the first time. Feeling confident, I skated a clean program, and landed both the loop and flip correctly.

If preparing for the competition hadn't totally convinced me that skating was to be my life, performing in front of an audience pulled me in hook, line, and sinker. There was something about being on the ice alone with people watching me, and then having them applaud afterwards, that I became instantly addicted to. Thriving on the attention, I could have performed for the audience all day. What inspired me just as much was receiving marks at the end of my program. It gave me an instant result that I could work to improve upon. However, it wasn't until my second competition, where I placed in the top three, that I realized there were medals and a podium to look forward to. Now, that was really exciting! I could be number one if I worked hard enough. I came fifth out of the 12 skaters at my debut competition, and couldn't wait for the next one.

During this period, I was still involved with other sports and activities, including ballet, volleyball, and swimming. My brother was also into various sports, and between the two of us, we kept our mother busy driving us to lessons and games. Finally, she told me I had to give something up. Apart from the expense, our schedules were making her crazy. I had no trouble dropping ballet immediately after my first skating competition. Even though I believe I would have made a half-decent ballerina, the excitement just wasn't there compared to figure skating.

I enjoyed volleyball, but didn't have the proper physique for the sport. I was too short and whenever I was at the net, I was unable to return the ball that was being driven over by someone almost twice my size. It bothered me that my team could lose because of my mistakes. I also had problems with my serve. No matter how hard I tried, I just couldn't get the ball over the net. Close to the end of one season, my team had somehow made the finals. Just before the big game, the coach promised to treat all of us to slush drinks if I could somehow manage to get the darn ball over the net while I was serving. When she made her offer, my eyes got so big. I thought, now you're talking! She should have said that at the beginning of the season. My very first serve went over the net.

Then there was swimming. Every morning before I went to the rink to skate, I took lessons at a neighbourhood pool. After learning the backstroke, my instructor told me to do two laps. I completed one, got out of the pool and said, "That's it! I'm swallowing too much water." I much preferred the frozen water of the ice rink.

Aiming for perfection, I always had to work hard at whatever I did. My brother, who also liked to be the best, took a different approach. While I studied for days before an exam to get good marks, Eric wouldn't do any homework and would still get an 80 percent grade. He wasn't lazy, but just had so much natural talent and intelligence. Still, it used to make me angry that I put everything into whatever I did and Eric could breeze through without much effort. When he was chosen to play for a double A hockey team, he discovered that some of the other boys were stronger than he was, which meant he would have had to work at being the best. So for the next few days, he didn't play well on purpose and was dropped one level, to a place where he already excelled and wouldn't have to struggle to keep up. My parents were told that he showed promise in tennis, but when Eric found out that he would have to play in tournaments, he quit. Too much work.

And I still laugh when I remember my brother taking figure skating lessons. Although the skating techniques he learned prepared him well for hockey, after a year in the sport he began to be teased by the other boys in school. Since figure skating required so much energy, the teasing and constant workload were probably getting to him. At his first and only competition, the music began to his one-minute program, but 30 seconds later, Eric was bowing, getting off the ice, and sitting on the bench, while his music continued to play on. He just wanted to do what he had to do and get off. A few months later, after practicing figure eights for a preliminary test, Eric wanted to leave the ice. His coach told him he had to do it again in front of the judges. He repeated the figures, but didn't wait for the judges, and was now determined to leave the ice. "It was their fault if they didn't see me," he reasoned. Eric's coach, who was inexperienced, began to cry in frustration. My dad insisted my brother take the test in front of the judges. So Eric took the test, but not before he informed everyone that if he passed, he would quit figure skating. He passed, and it was the last we saw of Eric at the rink. Not to say that my brother's way was wrong. Today he is a successful entrepreneur with his own business.

When I was about nine years old, the director of the club suggested that I should be skating more than once a week. By this time I had five badges to my credit, and my father, who was certain I was an absolute genius at the sport, decided to enrol me in summer school. So, I went from skating one day a week in a group to practicing five days a week with a private coach. It was like night and day. By the end of the summer, I was landing my Axel and was up to 12 badges. Of course, my father was beside himself with excitement. He heard of a smaller club that was also in Laval, called Les Lames d'Argent (Silver Blades). It only housed 200 skaters, which Dad thought would afford me more attention. He went to meet the president, who would also be the father of my future coach, Joanne Barbeau. My father told him I had great potential and bragged about how much talent I had. I am sure the president must have heard the same story from many parents, but maybe he saw a spark of something in me. He allowed me to join the club, where I would stay for the next 15 years.

Joanne and I instantly hit it off. We had a wonderful relationship and because she was only nine years older than me, we eventually became like sisters off the ice. On the ice, however, Joanne and I had a strict student/teacher relationship. I respected her and listened to everything she said.

Many of today's world-class skaters started in the sport before they were five. Because I began skating at such a late age, I was always playing catch-up with the other competitors. I would enter a competition, proud that I had learned my Lutz, and find the rest of the skaters executing Axels. So, the next competition I would have my Axel and double Salchow, but they would have double Salchows and double toes. Being a step behind the other skaters didn't discourage me. Rather, it made me more determined to succeed. I knew from the beginning that I liked to compete, so I worked to keep up and focused on individual goals that would prepare me for the next competition.

Skating three or four times a week in the winter, then five days a week in the summer, I learned all my double jumps by the time I was 10. That was fast. But unlike many young skaters, I wasn't afraid to jump. If a skater is nervous about jumping, she won't do a lot of stroking, which is the term for pushing yourself across the ice. If you aren't moving fast before you jump, there is more likelihood you will fall. But I loved speed. I still do. The feeling of the wind in my face thrilled me, and the more speed I had, the easier it was to jump. Of course, that's not to say that I didn't (and don't) fall down a lot. I've had more than my share of bruises.

My dad was probably my biggest fan, and became very involved in my skating. When video cameras first appeared on the market, he decided to check them out, planning to film me on the ice. My mother wasn't thrilled about him buying another new gadget, so he said he would just look at the new equipment. Then he winked at me behind her back. I felt like a co-conspirator, because I just knew my dad would purchase a camera. Thinking back, my mother probably knew too. Years later, we are so glad he made that purchase. We have four years of his face, voice, and actions on tape, and those memories are more precious than I can say.

Dad loved figure skating so much that he thought about becoming a judge. While I was having lessons, my father would be getting lessons of his own. Joanne would show me what to do and then explain to him what I was doing. This way, he recognized the various jumps, techniques, and movements. He actually became quite knowledgeable about the sport, and if he had lived I am certain he would have become involved at a higher level. Both my parents especially enjoyed the people at our club, who would treat the out-of-town competitions as mini-vacations. We travelled everywhere as a group, and it became like one close family.

Although my mother chauffeured me around, and even managed a few on-ice lessons when I started skating, she wasn't as taken with the sport as my dad. But it wasn't out of a lack of interest. As I mentioned, she was very protective of her children and often believed figure skating was too hard on me. She and my dad came to my competitions, but she didn't like to see me upset. Mom didn't mind watching Eric play hockey. She figured that if his team lost, they shared the experience together. However, in my sport, I was all by myself, and skating can be very lonely when you aren't doing well.

If I was having a difficult time, my parents reacted differently to my frustration or disappointment. Dad would say, "It's good for her. It builds character," while my mother couldn't bear to see me hurt. After my dad passed away, Mom began to volunteer with the club, and she would sometimes watch me practice. One day, while learning a new triple jump, I kept falling. I had landed it the day before, yet no matter how many times I tried, I couldn't seem to manage the jump again. I wouldn't stop, though. I was determined to land it. My mom called me over to the boards, patted me comfortingly on the back, and questioned what I was doing. "Why don't you just do single jumps?" she asked. "It doesn't matter to me if you are jumping triples. I just enjoy watching you skate."

I can recall being very upset with my mother on that day. Spoken out of love and admiration, her kind words were the last thing I needed to hear. It was during times like this when I especially longed for my father. As I prepared to land the jump again, I could almost hear him saying, "If you're tired of falling, no problem. Just stop falling! You did it yesterday, so do it again today." I think he would have given me the kick in the butt that we all need now and then.

My life would probably have been easier if my dad had been around. However, he taught me from an early age that determination is all-important if we want to succeed. As soon as you slow down, your ambition and drive will weaken. It's not good enough to think, "I'll only put 50 percent effort in today and 100 percent tomorrow." No matter what you do, you must give your all. Otherwise, you'll never see your true potential.

My father also taught me that we should do what we love to do, and the rewards will follow. I tried many different sports before I settled on skating. But when it became my passion, I devoted myself to it. Everything I did was 100 percent. I wouldn't allow myself to give any less. Of course, there were times when I didn't feel like being on the ice practicing. But on those days, I would work even harder. My face would be red with determination as I forced myself to do more. No one had to tell me to work. No one had to push me. I was there for one reason. I loved figure skating.

CHAPTER THREE

Getting Started is the Easy Part

Figure skating is a unique and multi-dimensional sport. Showcasing more than one talent in the athlete, it encompasses speed, movement, jumps, and rotation with both artistry and music. To skate at the international level takes great athletic and creative skills. It also takes years of practice. But you don't have to be aiming at a World Championship in order to participate in and enjoy the sport. There are thousands of people who take to the ice daily for exercise and fun. Whether you have dreams of standing atop the podium at a future Olympics, or simply want to meet your friends on the ice for an afternoon of pleasure, it all begins with the basics.

Scott Hamilton didn't start skating until he was eight years old. Kristi Yamaguchi was four, while Elizabeth Manley and Kurt Browning were three. The good news is, if you are taking up the sport for recreation, it won't make any difference how old you are. At 6 or 60, it is never too early or late to begin figure skating. World-class competitors, however, tend to begin the sport early in their lives, and probably wouldn't have reached a high level if they had started at a later time. Unless a skater is born with natural talent, it takes an average of three years to learn the double jumps necessary for organized competition. With that in mind, if someone begins skating at five, he or she could be into preliminary competitions by age eight, and at the junior national level in his or her teens.

To begin the sport at any age, the only equipment required is a pair of skates that are well-fitted and fabricated out of quality material. This is extremely important. If the first pair of skates is made of too strong a leather, the ankle won't move and blisters may form. On the other hand, the boots shouldn't be paper-thin, which is often the case with cheaper skates. If the leather is too thin, the skater can feel the blade underfoot, which is very uncomfortable. Furthermore, it may cause damage to the unsupported ankle. Gradually, the knees of the skater will turn in or out as the body attempts to compensate for the poor fit.

Although I have worn GAM skates for the past 10 years and have my own line of skates on the market, my first few pairs were either Donald Jackson's or Karen Magnussen's. They were ladies' figure skates purchased at a figure skating boutique. These stores specialize in the sport, and the personnel are trained to fit the foot expertly. It is not necessary for the boots to be custom-made, or even very expensive. A good first pair of skates shouldn't cost more than $100.

Young skaters tend to outgrow their boots quickly and usually require a couple of pairs a year, so another option would be second-hand skates. This is cost-effective, and offers the added advantage that the boot will already be broken in. From my own experience, there is nothing worse than trying to soften a new pair of boots. I will skate on my old ones for as long as possible before facing this headache (or should I say footache?). If you do choose to wear second-hand skates, I would again recommend visiting a specialty store that offers this alternative. While a used skate may be the right size, the fit around the anklebone may be different from the person who wore it before, which could spell extreme discomfort on the ice. Perhaps a better blade will be required for the boot. Either way, a trained professional will be able to personalize the skate to your foot. Once you are properly fitted for your first pair of skates, you will be more knowledgeable about how the second pair should fit.

To know if the skates are the correct size, you should be able to place one finger behind the heel. Any more space and the boot is too big. If the skate is too large and there is no other alternative, a thicker sock may be worn in the beginning. However, as the foot grows, a thinner sock should be worn. Too often I see parents pack their children's skates with layers of socks, believing it will keep them warm. Just the opposite is true.

Thicker socks will freeze against a tight boot, and the skater's feet will get colder.

I don't like the feeling of space in my skates, so I prefer a tighter boot, and I only wear tights on my feet while skating. If, for some reason, I have forgotten to bring my tights to practice, I will wear leggings and a thin pair of socks. With the skates fitting so snugly, they actually feel as if they are part of my body and allow me to move easily on the ice. Some skaters prefer wearing nothing inside their boots. Surya Bonaly and Brian Orser both go barefoot while skating. Because the foot doesn't slide, these skaters believe they have more control, which can be beneficial when landing a jump.

Bare feet wouldn't work for me, though. Perspiration causes the inside of my boots to become humid, and doesn't allow any flexibility when I want to change the position of my toes, a necessary action for certain moves and jumps. A thin sock or tights gives the small amount of slip that I require. Also, I believe that you are just asking for blisters and callouses by rubbing bare skin against leather. Even wearing tights, I can experience painful blisters that can only be healed by cutting a hole in my boot to alleviate the pain, or by taking a break from skating altogether.

While we are on the subject of skates, I am sometimes asked by curious novice skaters how often the blades should be sharpened. This is an individual decision. Some skaters I know like them done every week, while others prefer once every two months. And although this is not typical, World Champion Alexei Yagudin has his skates sharpened only once a year. I have mine done every two to three weeks. Jean-Michel sharpens them for me, and to tell you the truth, I don't feel any difference afterwards. If they were sharpened incorrectly, however, I would know immediately. Too sharp, and the skater can hit an edge and lose control. Too dull, and you are sliding all over the place.

You should also know how to lace up your skates correctly. They should be tightened from the arch of the foot at the first hook where the ankle bends. This way, the foot will be secure and the ankle area looser, which gives more flexibility and comfort. As the boots break in and get softer, the laces may be pulled a little tighter around the ankle.

If you've skated a few times and decide you like the sport, you may wish to take lessons. I believe the best way is to join a figure skating club. Although most cities across Canada have their own clubs, you could contact Skate Canada (formerly the Canadian Figure Skating Association, or CFSA) for more information if you are having difficulty locating one. Upon joining the club, the officials will offer you a list of amateur coaches from which to choose, and then they will place you in a group of people your own age. It may not be something you think about ahead of time, but trust me, teens and adults don't want to be taking lessons with five-year-olds, who may still be having trouble telling their left feet from their right. After awhile, if you are enjoying the sport and want to learn more, you may wish to sign up for private lessons.

For those parents who may be considering enrolling a young child in skating, please wait before paying for private lessons. Your child will probably become bored with one-on-one sessions with an adult, and the coach will take on the role of babysitter. By placing him or her in group lessons, however, the child will make new friends and have fun while learning the basics of skating. Normally, there is a half-hour of skating skills with the remaining time spent playing games on the ice. If the child shows interest in learning more after a year or two, he or she could then be enrolled in private lessons with an amateur coach.

You've purchased the skates, joined the club, and are ready to go. But what do you wear? Picture yourself bundled up on a snowy day. You're probably clad in boots, layers of undergarments and sweaters, a thick coat, hat, and scarf. Now envision yourself trying to walk on the ice outside with all those clothes on. Clumsy and awkward, isn't it? So why would you want to wear bulky clothing on an indoor ice rink while balancing on top of a couple of steel blades? It will be almost impossible to carry yourself and you will get tired faster. Instead, think light. Wear a pair of leggings, a cotton turtleneck to keep your neck warm, a pair of gloves, and a wool sweater, which is both warm and light. A couple of years ago, I performed a program called "The Sweater." My costume consisted of a skirt and oversized blue wool sweater, and in the program I executed several triple jumps. People asked how I could possibly jump in such a big and heavy costume. But it wasn't heavy at all. Because it was made of wool, it was almost weightless.

When working out on the ice, what you wear can make or break your practice. You have to be comfortable, or you'll want to pack it up and go home. I wear a tank top or bodysuit with Lycra tights because stretch is all-important. Overtop, I wear a sweatshirt for the first part of my practice until I become warm enough. If the rink is particularly cold, or if I'm practicing jumps and know that I will be falling a lot, I will also wear a pair of gloves to protect my hands.

One of the first things you'll learn when you begin to skate is how to fall and get back up again. Most novice skaters are afraid of falling, and rightfully so. The ice is a hard and slippery surface. But if you are going to skate, sooner or later you are going to fall. And when you begin jumping, tumbles on the ice will probably happen on a regular basis. You will get used to it, however. I've fallen so many times in my career that I don't even think about it. Most experienced skaters don't. When I fall now, I bounce right back up again, almost as if I was on a trampoline. And if I am in the middle of a competitive program and come crashing to the ice in a most unladylike manner, it usually hurts my ego much more than my body. But until you reach that level of experience, let me give you some pointers on the correct way to fall, which will hopefully minimize any danger.

To practice falling, put your hand in front of you, then gently go down on your knees. Lift one knee, put your foot down, and push yourself with your arms so you can place your other foot down. Then get up from there. After practicing this exercise many times, it will become automatic. Since this teaches the skater how to fall forward, it could prevent a future injury to the back or the head.

When inexperienced skaters initially step onto the ice, they tend to walk. This is only natural. So, one of the first movements you will learn is how to glide. Once you get used to the sensation, you will be taught how to push yourself from one end of the rink to the other. This is called stroking, and it is the very foundation of skating.

Stroking is the way to gain speed with elegance, and it's how you move from one place to another. As you go from element to element using crossovers, which is putting one foot across the other, stroking ties the package together. The best skaters will be able to move from one end of the rink to the other in one or two strokes. They move fast without looking as if they're working at it. There is forward stroking, (which is the first type you will learn, and what you will practice every day), backward stroking, counter-clockwise stroking, Russian stroking, and two-way stroking. All stroking begins with pumping your feet. Taking alternating steps, so that you are always skating on one leg, you push off from the inside edge of one skate, and then the inside edge of the other.

The concept of edges may seem complicated at first, but it's actually simple. Each skate blade has two edges: the inside edge and the outside edge. In the middle is a tiny groove that deepens depending on how sharp the blade is. While skating on a clean patch of ice, you will notice the edges on the surface. If you are skating flat, you will see two thin lines or tracks on the ice. If you are skating on one edge, only one line will be noticeable. Press on your big toe, lean slightly towards the inside of your leg, and you will be skating on an inside edge. Press on the small toe towards the outside of the leg, and you'll be on an outside edge. The edges of the blades are further divided into forward and backward edges. For example, if you are skating forward on an inside edge, you will be using the forward inside edge. Skating backwards on an outside edge, you will be using the back outside edge.

I can't stress enough that high-quality skating is all about edges. Skating flat, or on both edges of one blade, isn't considered to be good skating. You walk flat, so it is easy to skate flat. Skating on an edge, however, gives you speed, stability, and a smooth look as you glide across the ice.

Superior skating is also about bending the knees while stroking. You often hear the term "deep in the knees," which is used in reference to skaters who move across the ice in a powerful yet graceful manner. Bending the knees while stroking is the best way to maintain proper balance. European and Russian skaters are known for their deep-knee skating, as are many skaters of my generation and those that came before us. The overseas skaters have always been trained with an emphasis on stroking, while the skaters of my era grew up practicing figures. Figures were mandatory at competitions until 1992, when they were dropped. Although they were tedious to practice, figures refined our skating in a way that is not seen as much in the younger skaters, who tend to concentrate more on jumping than the basics of quality skating.

You'd think stopping on the ice would be easy. Actually, it is one of the more difficult elements to learn. Not only is it quite useful to know if you don't want to run into the boards or collide with another skater, but stopping fast can create some exciting moments in a skating program. Probably one of my most embarrassing moments – and I've had several – resulted from not stopping when I was supposed to. A couple of years ago, I was touring with "Stars on Ice." We were doing a group number to fast-paced music. Moving out onto the ice quickly, we were supposed to skate to the edge of the rink, make a big turn, and stop suddenly. The quick stop was especially effective because it caused snow to be thrown onto the audience members who sat in the front row.

Well, here we go. The cast races out, yelling and shouting. We turn, and everyone stopped but me. Because someone big was skating right behind me, I got nervous and instead of stopping, found myself sliding under the chair of a very large woman. Wedged in, I couldn't get out! I lay there for a moment staring at this poor lady's legs, and wondering how I get myself into these predicaments. Because it was a group number, the rest of the skaters just left me under the chair as they went into their various routines. Thank goodness, Barbara Underhill took pity on me. She forgot about her own number and came to my rescue, helping to pull me out from under the chair. So much for grace and elegance on the ice.

There are a few ways to stop, but they all use the same theory of turning the blades of your skates sideways to slow you down. Practicing the "skid," also called the "snowplow," with just one foot is the quickest way to learn. Turn your foot in by pushing on your big toe, then push the blade of your skate away from you. This will make a little pile of snow, similar to the way you stop in skiing. When you become comfortable doing this on one foot, try it using both feet.

The two most common ways of turning on the ice are called the "Mohawk" and the "three turn." Used to reverse from forward to backward skating, they also precede certain jumps. As a beginner, you will want to start on two legs and when you get the hang of the turn, graduate to one leg. A three turn gets its name from the way the etching looks on the ice after you have finished. It sort of resembles the number three, although I think of it as a flying bird. Moving forward with your knees bent, pull your left arm forward and your right arm back. As you begin to turn, reverse your arms. The difference with a Mohawk turn (maybe it is called that because if you use your imagination, the tracings are similar to a Mohawk haircut) is that you change to your other foot as you are turning.

There is nothing that feels quite so wonderful as finally landing a jump that you have practiced for months. However, the thought of leaping into the air, turning, and coming back down safely can be scary. To get acquainted with the sensation of leaving the ice, you will be taught a bunny hop jump before any others. This exercise teaches you how to bring your free leg up into the air, land on your toe, and glide, with no rotation involved. After the bunny hop is accomplished, the next step is mastering the waltz jump. This is a half-rotation, and is similar to the more difficult Axel, which we will discuss in the next chapter.

That brings us to what is probably the most beautiful element of women's figure skating: spinning. There is something magical about a well-executed spin. Watch Lucinda Ruh of Switzerland as she performs magnificent pirouettes at a breathtaking speed, and you will see what I mean. Scott Davis of the United States is a master at spinning. He rotates so fast that his entire body becomes a blur. For excitement and beauty, there is nothing like a good spin.

All spins are either flying – meaning they have a jump in the beginning – or non-flying. Some of the non-flying spins are the upright, layback, camel, and sit spin, while flying spins include the camel, death drop, and flying sit spin. To get the sensation of turning and a feel for where the middle is, start on two feet with your arms at your sides. Bring one leg up and bend the knee. Then lift it up further so your boot is level with the other knee. By standing like this, you will become aware of how your arms will help centre you in a spin. If you spin with your arms out, you won't rotate very fast. As soon as you bring them in to your body, however, you gain the necessary speed. That also includes your legs; the tighter together they are, the faster you will spin.

This pretty much covers the rudiments of skating, but please keep in mind that these and any other instructions I present to you in this book are meant only to give you a general knowledge of the sport. Probably the most valuable advice I could offer is to listen to your coach at all times. Unlike those in many other countries, individuals who teach skating in Canada have gone through many levels of accreditation. Canadian coaches have the wisdom, skills, and experience to demonstrate proper technique. And in all my years of skating, I am proud to say that I have never talked back to any of my coaches. They have been there to teach and guide me, and I respect their knowledge immensely. This is not to say that if you are experiencing difficulties with a coach, you shouldn't change after giving it careful consideration. What works for you at 5 may not work for you at 15. But above all, have fun on the ice. Remember, that's why you started skating in the first place!

CHAPTER FOUR

So You Want to Compete

The more involved a person becomes with skating, the more serious the game gets. Competition is now one of the main focal points of the sport, and the strategy becomes very different. Instead of just having family or a few people from the club watching you skate, there is an audience in the stands. And the further you climb through the ranks, the larger that audience gets. There will also be a panel of individuals who judge your every move on the ice. More forgiving of mistakes made by the inexperienced skater, a judge's tolerance will rapidly decline as your commitment to the sport grows.

Competition at the higher level is not to be taken lightly. The training is demanding, the hours are long, and it all costs money. Consequently, the desire to compete must be strong in order to achieve any measure of success. However, there should still be a great deal of enjoyment and fun in the process. You must retain the passion. Without it, you won't get far.

At this stage, you've been through the inter-club competitions, where you went up against skaters that you were quite familiar with since you trained alongside them every day. Perhaps you've tried some regional competitions against other skaters in the area. But something about the competitive arena lit a fire deep inside. You want to go on to a sectional competition that pits the best of the province against one another and gets you noticed by Skate Canada. To perform well here means a chance to skate at the Nationals.

Now is the time to ensure that your coach has a clear understanding of your ambition. Many coaches are only interested in teaching and have no wish to follow the skater from competition to competition. If this is the case, they should recommend another coach who wants to go as far in the skating world as you do. That person should be someone who you admire and respect, yet still feel comfortable talking to about your worries, doubts, and frustrations. But you should never become too close. A line may be crossed and the respect that is so necessary between a teacher and a student could be lost. Although my second coach, Joanne, and I were friendly off the ice, she kept her distance while we were training. Because of this, I never lost sight of the fact that she was first and foremost my teacher. So many times, I've heard skaters mouth off to their coaches, which I believe shows a total lack of respect. They're tired, irritable, and don't want to continue with practice. If I was running through my program and stopped in the middle, Joanne would quickly assess the situation. Unless I was ill or injured, I knew I'd get an order to keep going. I had faith in her judgment and did what I was told.

Many coaches have previous competitive skating experience. Ideally, you want to be taught by someone with a good technique. Although that's difficult to determine before beginning lessons, you could watch the person teaching other students or get a recommendation from someone you trust. With a background in physical education, Joanne was a skater before she became a coach. Her skating technique was excellent and she passed these skills on to me. By watching her, I landed a triple toe jump clean the first time out. Handling my off-ice training until I was well into the junior level, she instilled a regimen in my training pattern that I still use today.

Once you're comfortable with your coach, you should start early to form a good base in skating that will serve you well over the coming years. It's easy to fall into bad habits, and then very difficult to break them later on. The tricks become more risky and demanding as you advance, and a good practice routine is required from the start.

I had a strong sense of self-discipline from an early age, and because of this I never had a hard time telling my friends that I couldn't go out with them in the evenings because I was practicing the next morning. When I began to compete more intensively, I skated and trained almost every day. I learned early on that the better shape I was in, the more agile I was on the ice. If I spent too much time away from the rink or gym, it showed up quickly. In fact, statistics prove that after only three days away from any exercise program, a person will begin to lose strength and flexibility.

I was fortunate enough to be enrolled in a school that allowed me and the other students to set our own schedules and progress as individuals, and as a result I was able to put in the hours I needed at the rink. Rising early in the morning, I'd work out from 5:30 to 6:30, take a shower, and be on the bus by 7:00. Arriving at school by 8:00, I would take classes until noon, when my mother would pick me up and drive me to the rink. I would skate from 12:30 to 4:30, then catch a ride back home to eat dinner and do homework. At least two nights a week, I would head back to the rink for further practice. I usually took Saturdays off, believing that my body required one day a week to recuperate. On those days, I'd shop or participate in an outdoor activity. On Sundays, I skated for an hour, then worked out lightly so my muscles wouldn't go into shock on Monday morning, when my vigorous routine would start all over again. During the summer, I skated six hours a day, five days a week.

You often hear of athletes dropping out of school to fully concentrate on a sport, in the hopes they will someday make a career out of it. I don't believe anyone should give up his or her education for this reason. Being an Olympic or World Champion may be your goal, but it is not reality. A diploma is something concrete that can be relied upon long after the skating ends. Not only does a person need these credentials to ensure a better future, but going to school maintains a healthy balance. You need to see and experience all aspects of life and build relationships outside of the rink. Even though it took me four years to finish three years of high school because of the time I missed for competition, I would do it all over in a heartbeat. There were periods when I was under so much pressure in my skating that returning to school and concentrating on my studies was a pleasure. I'm still in school now. I know there will be a life after skating, so a couple of years ago, I enrolled part-time to study fashion design.

Because I loved being on the ice, I never had a problem with the skating side of my training. However, off-ice workouts were another story. I tried everything from ballet to karate to improve my flexibility and strengthen the core of my body. Although I would begin the programs with the best of intentions, within two or three weeks, I'd lose interest. Any exercise other than skating wasn't fun to me. I'd persist at whatever it was I was supposed to do, but only to gain advantage on the ice.

I did a lot of weight training as a teenager, and it wasn't until after I turned professional that I realized weights weren't for me. Through skating, and also because of the way I am built, my body already had the power and muscle. It was my cardiovascular system that needed work. I wish I had realized this earlier on because I always had to push to get through the last $1^1/2$ minutes of a 4-minute program. Anything that called for exerting myself in a short amount of time was easy for me. I was fast and jumped with little effort. I could also rotate quickly. Using weights, however, curtailed my endurance because of all the power I used for one jump. After two or three jumps, I would tire and have difficulty getting through the rest of the program. When I left the amateur ranks, I discovered jogging, and it vastly improved my stamina. Some female skaters do require weight training, however. Kristi Yamaguchi is a good example. Her body is built differently than mine. Whereas I develop muscle easily, Kristi's smaller frame once lacked the strength to attain higher jumps. Weight training was one of the ways she gained power and went on to win an Olympic gold medal.

Since becoming a professional skater, my training habits have been modified to accommodate the busy lifestyle I lead. From September to March for five days a week, I now practice skating for two hours and train for another hour off the ice. If I'm performing on a weekend, then I will also train on those days. Recently, I have started toning exercises. In my thirties now, I've had to face the fact that gravity happens! Last year I was on a tour in which I found myself to be one of the oldest skaters. Most of the cast were still amateur and training year-round for international competitions. Their bodies were sleek and well-toned, reflecting the many hours of training they endured. One day I was in the dressing room, complaining in a lighthearted way that I was losing my natural firmness. To prove my point, I gave my rear a little shake and said, "See, it's just like Jell-O!"

It took me a long time to develop a sense of humour about my body. Years ago, I would have been horrified to see even an ounce of fat. Now I can laugh. I'm much kinder to myself these days. Besides, I'm skating better than I ever have. My muscle is natural and doesn't weigh me down on the ice. And if I do feel a little depressed when I notice another part of my body drooping or getting soft, I just remember that Jell-O is lighter than pound cake.

While building muscle is almost effortless for me, I have always had to work on my overall flexibility. When I was seven, and fellow skaters were learning the splits in a few weeks, it took me a year to be able to coax my body into that painful position. It doesn't come naturally to me, yet keeping myself limber is an essential part of my training because it may prevent an on-ice injury. While you won't see me pulling my leg up behind my head while spinning, at least I can do a graceful spiral without pulling a groin muscle. Some skaters carry their flexibility workouts a little further and will stretch before going on the ice. I'm not one of them, as I'm uncertain whether it's of any benefit. Sometimes the more flexible a skater is, the less explosive his or her jumps may be on the ice because muscles don't often respond well to an intensive warm-up. However, I look at skaters like Michelle Kwan and Sarah Hughes, both of whom are extremely pliant and able to maintain their strength. I think it is all in the way you are built.

While there is no time limit to learn the required jumps, the earlier a person begins working on these elements the better. I was able to execute my first Axel before I was 10, and the following year I had mastered the double jumps. I landed a triple Salchow by the time I was 14, but it took me a little longer to land the double Axel, which is a more difficult jump. With practice, I was able to do most of the triples before I was 15. I was considered a fast learner, yet Midori Ito of Japan had conquered many of the triple jumps by the ripe old age of eight!

There are six jumps that have to be learned if you want to keep up with the rest of your competitors. They are taught in this order: the Axel, Salchow, toe, loop, flip, and Lutz. All jumps are either toe- or edge-assisted. The edge jumps, which include the Axel, Salchow, and loop, are so called because the skater takes off on one of the four edges of the blade. The toe, flip, and Lutz are toe-assisted jumps, meaning the skater uses the toe pick of the blade to push into the air. Because the Axel consists of an extra half-rotation, it is considered to be the most challenging jump to learn. While all jumps are landed backwards, the Axel also differentiates itself from the others because it is the only jump in which the skater takes off while going forward.

When I was learning to jump, many of the skaters wore falling pads to protect their hips and rear ends. Harnesses were another method used in an attempt to teach the skater the various jumps. Although I used both devices for a short while in order to the get the feel of the jumps, I am not a big believer in either of the apparati. It is too easy to become dependent on them. When they are removed and the skater has to go it alone, he or she may be frightened of falling and suddenly change technique. Use them for awhile if you must, but don't rely on them. Sooner or later, you have to trust in your own natural reflexes.

I can understand people being afraid to fall. But when you do miss a jump, you should get up and try it again. If you're practicing your program and fall in the middle of it, continue on with the rest of the number. But after you've finished, try the jump again. Fight through the fear immediately, because putting it off will only increase your anxiety. If you find yourself still having trouble with a particular jump that you've already learned, don't push yourself to the point where your body tightens up. As you tense, you will lose all feeling for the jump. Instead, go back to the basics.

I can recall having trouble with a double Lutz during one training session. I fell so many times that I hurt my head in the same spot twice in a span of 45 minutes. After awhile, my body began to tighten, and I should have stopped. But I was stubborn and unafraid, and I continued to throw myself into the air. The falls I sustained that day eventually resulted in a severe back injury. The next morning, I was still having trouble with the jump, so I went back to square one. Starting on a flat surface, I practiced a single Lutz in my running shoes. And in no time at all, I was back on the ice doing the double. I call these back-to-the-basic sessions "walk-throughs." If you're having trouble with a triple jump, start over with a single, then a double before you try the triple. Make sure your muscles and ankles are warmed up and practice the rotation first. Then run through the technique. If you can do them together, great. But be careful. Landing a jump is much easier on the ice, where you are able to slide. If you don't do the jump correctly off-ice, you could easily twist an ankle by attempting the full jump.

I found the trampoline to be a useful asset for learning my jumps. Besides being good for the abdominal muscles, it also helped me to become more aware of my centre, which assisted in my jumping ability. Because you have to stay in the middle of the trampoline in order to stay on, you become familiar with where you are supposed to be in the air as you jump. While on the trampoline, however, please remember that jumps are meant to be vertical, not horizontal. It may sound obvious, but it's easy to tilt in the air, which could cause a serious tumble off the trampoline.

When skaters first begin competing at the club level at the ages of seven or eight, they will most likely be in the pre-juvenile group. At 9, 10, and 11, they will have moved on to juvenile, then pre-novice. By the time they reach their teens, they will probably be at the novice level. From there, they move to junior, and finally to senior. While there is no age limit for seniors, to make it to a Junior World competition, the female skater must be 18 before July 1st and the male must be 19. I never made it to Junior Worlds. In my day, the age limit was 16, and because I was off the ice for several months following a back injury, I was too old to participate by the time I qualified.

Getting from a small inter-club competition to a major international one involves many small steps. I never looked ahead or dreamed about competing at a World Championship or Olympics when I was young. Somehow, I just couldn't put myself in that picture. Instead, I concentrated on short-term goals. I went from month to month and from year to year. I still plan that way. I like to set my sights on where I want to be at the end of the week, and then at the end of the month. As I mentioned earlier, if any of the other skaters had more jumps than I did when I went to competitions, I would ensure I had those jumps ready for the next competition.

However you go about setting your schedule, you must have a plan. Start in the summer by looking at the overall picture. Decide what your main competition of the season will be, and then work backwards from there. For example, when the Canadian National Championships were my priority, I knew I had to be ready for the competition by mid-December since they were held in early January. So my coach and I would sit down and figure out a game plan. It's important that your programs be routine three weeks prior to the actual date of the major competition. Unless it's absolutely necessary, nothing should be changed during this period. Practice only to maintain the program.

Late spring and early summer is the time period when your programs are put together for the season. You and your coach may have already selected the music, and over the next few months you will learn the new choreography, jumps, footwork, spins, and spirals that will eventually be woven together to create your competitive programs. It is an intensive period of training because you are using many different muscles. As you come close to your first competition, the training becomes even more intense, but shorter and more specific as problem areas are worked on. Although the summer hours of training are long as skaters try to broaden their repertoire, it is also a creative period with time spent on developing artistry and transition movements. I have always looked at the summer as a new beginning, full of interesting ideas and exciting possibilities.

Although I enjoy all types of music, from reggae to pop to country to rock, I don't necessarily select my competitive music based on my own favourites. There have been times when I haven't been thrilled with a particular song that my coach or choreographer wanted me to perform to, but changed my mind when I tried skating to the piece. The acoustics in a skating rink are different than in your living room. There is echoing and a change in sound that can say something to your body when you move on the ice. Other times, I have loved a certain piece of music that my coach may have objected to, only to find that it wasn't suitable to skate to. In 1992, I found a song that I desperately wanted for one of my programs. I brought it to the attention of Joanne, who didn't like it. However, she told me to go ahead and try it on the ice. As usual, my coach was right. The music was beautiful, but I couldn't skate to it. Although I always have the last say in what music I will be performing to, I have found it best to listen to the experts.

I adore Latin music, and although I performed to it one year, I don't think I was all that believable playing a Spanish temptress. Someone like Lu Chen can interpret this type of music far better than me because of the seductive way she skates. It's the same with blues music, or any type of song for which I have to portray someone sultry or sexy. My personality is more bubbly and fun, and if I take myself too seriously, I will be tripping all over the ice within 10 seconds.

During "Stars on Ice" one year, I had to do a vamp number with Shae-Lynn Bourne. Thank goodness it was a short routine, because I was very uncomfortable. I almost found it embarrassing. Let's face it, I'm not built like Shae-Lynn, Katarina Witt, and many of the other tall female skaters. To be perfectly blunt, I'm flat-chested. I'm not alone, though. Quite a few of us shorter skaters are not overly endowed in this area. I'll let you in on a little secret. If you ever see me on the ice and it looks like I've suddenly developed a chest, it is the result of things we call "cookies." Drop these things down the front of our costumes, and voilà – we're suddenly voluptuous!

Every now and then, skaters will turn up at the same competition with the same music. In the 2000/2001 season, Alexei Yagudin and Elvis Stojko both skated to "Gladiator." Probably the most memorable competition where this happened was at the 1988 Olympics, when both Debbi Thomas of the United States and Katarina Witt of Germany skated to "Carmen." I don't know what I would have done in this same situation, but I think if I learned that a major competitor was skating to the same music as me, I would change my program. However, this is when having your own identity comes into play.

When you reach a certain level of competition, it is absolutely necessary to make yourself stand out from the other skaters. And the best way to do that is to let your personality shine while you are performing. Be an individual. Wear a costume that has been designed just for you and interpret the music the way you feel it. Don't copy another skater who has come before you. This way, even if you do show up at a competition with the same music as someone else, the one with the better skating technique, artistic presentation, and overall package will win.

When you are young, your coach will create your programs. But as you begin to take competition more seriously, a good choreographer is very important to your career. You can't see yourself on the ice the way others see you, and a trained choreographer will be able to help develop programs that are true to your own unique style. I've worked with many of the top choreographers over the years, including Lori Nichol, Lea-Ann Miller, David Wilson, and Sandra Bezic. And although I will do my own choreography if I am performing in a smaller show such as a Christmas or Halloween special, I much prefer working with someone else. I can be more creative when a professional is guiding and helping me through the process. On my own, I'm not as confident. Designing costumes is a different story. After years of working with the best in the business, and because of my own love of fashion, I am very comfortable coming up with the ideas as to what I'll wear while performing.

The right costume is an integral part of the look a skater is attempting to portray on the ice. Yes, the judges are marking us based on our skating abilities and creativity, but because figure skating is such a subjective sport, they are also judging us on how we look. Right or wrong, and like any other area in life, what we wear often forms a lasting impression on those around us. When first competing, many skaters will go to a figure skating boutique and select a dress off the rack. But because most skaters don't want to turn up at a competition and have several other skaters wearing the same dress, they will add trim, beads, a scarf, or a jacket to individualize the outfit. Others will have their dresses made by a parent or friend. Using my designs, my mother made many of my costumes and all my practice outfits until I was competing as a junior. Because judges and other important people would show up for our daily practices, we had to wear a different outfit every day. In all, I would require six or seven practice dresses and three costumes for the competitive programs, since figures were still being judged back then. My poor mother couldn't keep up, and because I hated trying outfits on, we would argue during the fittings. Mom figured the time and money spent, as well as my constant complaining, wasn't worth it. Before long, she sent me to a seamstress.

I was fascinated with the idea of clothing design from the moment I walked into the seamstresses' establishment. Losing track of time, I would stay for hours and watch the ladies work. I played with the sparkly beads and was awestruck by the multitude of fabrics and colours. If the seamstress had to shop for a certain type of fabric, I would go along with her. After awhile, I realized she was making at least 200 costumes a year, and had no time for creativity. Because I wanted my dresses to look a certain way, I began sketching my ideas on paper and turning them over to her to produce. I wanted to be involved in every aspect and would even visit the man who specialized in dying the costumes. Because the procedure was still experimental, it was quite fascinating to watch. Using a blow-dryer, he would heat areas of the costume until they changed from a dark to a light colour. One of my favourite outfits was done in this manner. A dark pink colour ran through the skirt, faded to a lighter pink near the top, and paled to white at the shoulders. It was stunning.

I continued to design my own costumes until I moved to Toronto in 1993. Then I began to work with a variety of costume designers, including the famed Francis Defoe, who also happens to be a judge. I think the costume designer I most admire, however, is Jeff Billings. Besides creating the multitude of costumes for "Stars on Ice," Jeff is known for designs that have graced the Broadway stage, and he has created numerous ensembles for movie stars attending award shows such as the Oscars. Because he knew of my interest in costume design, Jeff would talk to me about his creations while we were rehearsing and getting fittings for Stars. Over a period of time, he taught me how to cut skirts and let me in on many tips of the trade. I'm a far cry from a Jeff

Billings, but along with coaching, I eventually want to concentrate on fashion design on a full-time basis, and am currently helping other skaters with their own costumes.

The higher a skater goes competitively, the more expensive the costume becomes. Because the range of colours is limited in the stretch material required for a good fit, fabrics have to be dyed, and that costs money. Beads and sequins are sewn on by hand to ensure the tiny decorations stay in place. Add the hours spent designing, sewing, and fitting the outfit, and it can run the skater anywhere from $500 to $5,000. Quebec skaters are the most fortunate when it comes to cost. Since many of the women in the province had children in figure skating, several of them took to making costumes. There is now an abundance of seamstresses in Quebec and prices are lower there than anywhere else in the country. Skaters from Ontario will often go to the National Ballet to have their costumes made. However, their prices are high since you are paying for the name and experience.

Far more goes into costume-making than just how it will look on the ice. After all, you will be leaping, twisting, turning, and getting into all sorts of unnatural positions while performing. Accordingly, a costume should be fit quite closely to your body, but you should be able to move with it. You don't want anything ripping while you are in mid-air. Furthermore, the material should be light enough that it allows the body to breathe.

I can remember one year when Jean-Michel was preparing for one of the first competitions of the season. He had an outfit made that was supposed to resemble a suit, and although it wasn't one of my favourites, he rather liked it. Halfway into the competition, Jean-Michel absolutely died on the ice. He just couldn't carry on. Worried that something was physically wrong with him, I rushed to his side as he approached the boards. He looked at me and muttered, "That's the first and last time I will be wearing this outfit." The costume had too many layers and was made out of a heavy material. As a pairs skater, Jean-Michel exerts huge amounts of energy as he lifts and throws his partner, and this particular costume wouldn't allow his body to breathe underneath. He quickly tired and had to stop.

I once had a practice skirt made out of a slinky ribbed material. It was longer than what I was accustomed to, but I wanted something different. Thank goodness I wasn't wearing it for a competition! Every time I attempted a jump, the skirt wrapped itself around my legs and I couldn't stop myself from rotating. It whipped around me in a frenzy and threw off my timing entirely.

I think my all-time favourite costume was the one I wore skating to "Moon River," when I won my first Canadian professional title. The black dress with white trim was elegantly simple, and with my hair twisted back, I felt like Audrey Hepburn, the character I was portraying on the ice. Even though I like to feel pretty while performing, I don't always dress in such a sophisticated manner. Last year, I skated to "Humouresque," and in my white-faced makeup and Harlequin outfit, I felt downright ugly standing next to the other girls before our warm-up. But I was playing a mime and believed it was necessary to dress the part. Because it was a pro-am competition, I was up against Michelle Kwan and other women who were still eligible skaters (meaning they were still eligible to compete in the Olympics). Although Michelle and I fared about the same technically, I moved ahead with my creative marks and won the competition.

And just a word about caring for costumes. Because colours can run, and beading and chiffon are delicate, I never trust my outfits to a dry cleaner, or anyone else for that matter. The costumes are too expensive to take a chance on someone ruining them. Besides, if anything should go wrong, it isn't as if you can magically conjure up another ensemble in a week or two. So I wash them myself, by hand, ensuring they'll be in top shape when I need them.

By September or October, your programs, costumes, and choreography should all be in place. Your first competition of the season is looming, and it will be important because the results will tell you where you are with your training, and what more you need to achieve. If at all possible, it is wise to perform in a simulated competition first. We call this "breaking the ice." Gathering as many people for the audience as you can, and a judge if at all plausible, you will run through your programs exactly as if you were at a major competition. Sometimes it's not possible to have an audience or a judge, so you have to make believe that the crowd is in the stands. My coach and I would go so far as to have me skate a six-minute warm-up, then pretending we had drawn to see the order of skate. If I drew third, I would sit and wait while the imaginary skaters ahead of me completed their routines. Then I would skate as if I were performing in front of an international panel of judges.

When you do get to your first competition of the season, it is important to listen to the judges. You may have been very creative in the summer but inadvertently put an illegal move into your technical program. It may be something as irrelevant as coming out of a spin on the wrong foot. Whatever the unsanctioned manoeuvre, if it is not in the rule book, the judges will mark you down and later tell you or your coach to take the element out. Pay attention to and respect the judges. There is no point in arguing with any of them. And the judge with whom you may be most annoyed could be sitting on the panel at a future competition you're in, armed with the deciding vote.

Mentally preparing for a competition can be just as challenging as physical preparation. The method used by most skaters is visualization. Visualizing how you will look and feel on the ice takes a lot of practice, and you should begin early in the summer. It may be difficult to picture yourself landing the new jumps and performing unfamiliar footwork, but as your programs come together, so will your visualization. Play your programs over and over again in your mind. I would even visualize my warm-up routine, which was always the same. In my head, I could see myself skating the length of the rink forwards and then backwards. I knew I would be stroking more than the rest of the skaters because I needed to get the feel of the ice. I always started with a waltz jump, then right into a double Salchow, which has always been the key jump for me. Because the Salchow is an edge jump, I would know right away if I was making solid contact with the ice. If I had good timing with my edges, the toe jumps would come easy. A few seconds later I would execute a double Axel and then a triple Salchow. I could also imagine what the other competitors would be doing in their own warm-ups. Michelle Kwan, for example, always stroked first and then went into spirals, while Yuka Sato practiced her footwork.

I would also visualize the waiting period. For instance, through one visualization, I would tell myself I was the second competitor to skate, and would then imagine the waiting time. It was necessary for me to visualize this segment of the competition because, until I learned better, I used to stand while waiting for fear that my legs would get soft. I had so much energy that I'd become hyper, feeling as if I could jump over a house.

During my first year as a senior, I was competing at a sectional competition and was determined to become the Quebec champion. I was so wound up with anticipation that when the announcer called my name, I raced across the ice to get into position. In the process I stepped on my blade. Both my feet went forward, and the next thing I knew I was on my butt. The program hadn't even started! The judges, audience, and even my coach were laughing so hard they had tears rolling down their cheeks. But that was me – always in a hurry to get started.

Visualization shouldn't end with the completion of your program. Picture yourself bowing to the audience, sitting in the "kiss-and-cry," and receiving fantastic marks. Then go so far as to imagine yourself on the top rung of the podium. If you repeatedly practice this method, then follow through with it while performing, the end result will come very close to what you have pictured. Even if you don't win – or even place – at a competition, if you have done everything that you mentally imagined yourself doing, then you know you have skated your absolute best at that given moment. That in itself can be as satisfying as winning.

Nerves used to be my worst enemy prior to a competition, and I was about 12 years old when they first hit me. I remember my coach telling me to imagine the judges were clad in nothing but patterned boxer shorts. It worked for a time, and I would even compete with a grin on my face. But as the years wore on, the anxiety grew, and my childhood imaginings didn't solve the problem. It got so bad that the night before any major competition, I would dream that I was skating my program non-stop, and wake up exhausted in the morning. Even now, I tend to get emotional and on edge before a major competition. I think my family and friends will tell you that I'm not the best person to be around during this time.

In 1993, when I was about to skate my long program that would earn me my second Canadian title, I stayed up all night fighting with Jean-Michel, who had already finished his competition. I wanted him with me during the evening, but he had other obligations with his partner. Because my nerves were raw and I was concentrating only on myself, I lashed out at him when we finally caught up with each other. Wanting to settle the argument before I went to bed, I can remember some pretty serious yelling going on in the hotel hallway. Poor Jean-Michel. Nothing he said made any difference, and I went to bed determined that I wasn't going to let him affect my skating. The following day, I didn't speak to him at all. Arriving at the rink, I realized that I didn't have my toothpaste with me. Most skaters rub a little of the substance inside their mouths to keep them from getting dry. Jean-Michel ran to the store to get me a tube and I didn't even thank him. I went on the ice, stubborn and determined. But I won the championship. Afterwards,

I hugged and kissed Jean-Michel as if nothing had happened. No doubt about it, I'm totally impossible to be around before a competition.

I tried everything to calm my nerves before a major event, from visualization to sleeping. Some skaters will read and others will work on creative projects. Isabelle Brasseur and Elizabeth Manley are both known for the beautiful sweaters they knit while waiting to compete or perform. Although I like to do embroidery, I believe I have finally found a way to totally relax myself before stepping on the ice. I go shopping. Even if I only have a half-hour before I'm supposed to be at the rink, I will head to the mall or the hotel shops. In the stores, I'm in another world and forget about everything as I shop for anything from nail polish to furniture. And I hate leaving the stores empty-handed. Even if I only have purchased a pair of socks or a new lipstick, I have to come out with something. What can I say? It works for me!

I've had many ups and downs in my competitive career. There were times when I was devastated with the results of a competition, and couldn't focus on anything except the negative. Please believe me when I tell you that it just isn't worth it. I never won an Olympics. Neither did Toller Cranston, Brian Orser, Kurt Browning, or a multitude of other skaters. Yet, for all of the upset and doubt it caused us at the time, we went on to successful professional careers. If I had only known then what I know now, I would have saved myself a lot of grief and emotional upheaval. Life doesn't revolve around how well you do at a competition. Good or bad, it is all just experience. You just have to learn how to turn the page and move on.

CHAPTER FIVE

Change Happens

On New Year's Eve, 1981, my life changed forever. It's funny, because just a few months earlier, things couldn't have been more normal. It was the summer I turned 12. My parents were thinking of buying a new home, and although I was excited at the prospect, as usual, my mind was focused on skating.

There was an out-of-town competition scheduled in August, and as was our custom, the entire family went for the weekend. I don't remember how I placed at the event, but I do recall what a good time we had. My parents mixed with their friends, who also had children in the competition, and there was much laughter by the hotel pool. On the way home, my dad didn't feel well and my mother urged him to see a doctor. But he brushed away her concerns. About a week later, he felt even worse and finally consented to go to the hospital. After days of testing, my father was diagnosed with intestinal cancer. He was 36 years old.

They operated and Dad was released from the hospital in October. Within a short time, however, he was readmitted. The cancer had spread. Eric and I visited him regularly, but we weren't allowed to see him the week before he died. I think my mother was trying to shelter us from the ravages of his disease, and our last opportunity to be with him came at Christmas. We were told he was in a coma and was unaware of his surroundings, yet when I pulled on his hand, he gave me a sign of recognition and gently squeezed my hand back. My father passed away on December 31st, the eve of his birthday, and I've missed him every day since.

My mother tried to keep our lifestyle the same afterwards. She insisted we go to school, see our friends, and carry on with our other activities. But it was very difficult because she wasn't the same person. While my father was ill, she spent most of her time at the hospital and grew increasingly tired and nervous. Probably remembering the trauma of losing her own father when she was nine, Mom tried to hide the severity of my dad's illness from us. We never quite knew what was going on. Then after he died, the three of us behaved as if he were still alive. My mother continued to set the table for four, and Eric and I told our classmates that our father was away on business. We were in total denial.

Deep down, I knew my father had died. I was at his funeral and I saw him. I guess I just didn't want to believe it. But instead of talking about it, we acted as if nothing had happened. We didn't want to let him go. I can remember worrying about my mother, but I was afraid to ask her how she was faring. It was all I could do to look after myself. I just didn't want to hear any more bad news. I was also anxious about whether we had the finances to continue my skating. But I never asked. Our denial was an unhealthy situation that went on for quite some time. My mother finally went to seek professional help after a teacher called to inform her that Eric and I were continually speaking about our dad as if he were alive. Mom realized she needed to get better for us.

It's painful for me to look back on this now because it evokes such disturbing memories. However, I learned so much from this experience. Because I didn't talk about my feelings during this distressing time, the grief came out in other ways. For example, I became angry and bitter. We knew another man who had the same type of cancer my father had. He survived and I couldn't understand why God allowed him to live, yet let my dad die. I also became very selfish. Because I wanted to believe that my father was coming back, I made it difficult for my mother to have any kind of social life. I didn't want her seeing anyone outside of the family because I was afraid she would meet another man.

Bottling everything up also affected my health. I avoided sleep because I cried during the night. So instead, I went non-stop. If I was quiet or alone, I would think too much, so I surrounded myself with people and skated more than ever. Two years after my dad died, I began to experience severe stomach cramps that caused me to faint. The doctors told my mother I might have leukemia. I can't even imagine how she must have felt when they dropped this bombshell. The ailment turned out to be an infection in the intestines that eventually led to mononucleosis. Although I had a bit of a setback when I became allergic to the sulpha drug I'd been prescribed, I was back on my feet in three weeks. I do believe, however, that my illness was a direct result of the emotional pain I was suffering.

It took me over 10 years to fully come to terms with losing my father at such an early age. Before he died, I was outgoing and never anxious on the ice. Afterwards, I began to put such intense pressure on myself to do well that I often sabotaged my performances. It wasn't until 1996, when I finally talked to a therapist, that I realized something very startling. Shortly after my dad died, I had secretly vowed that I would succeed for him. Later, if I didn't perform up to par at a competition, I felt like I was letting him down, and would beat myself up for it. This led to depression and even feelings of shame. It was an awfully big promise for a little girl to make, and it certainly took its toll.

My dad would never have wanted me to go through this. He so loved to watch me skate, and when I think back, his love had nothing to do with whether I won a competition or came in

Josée's mother,
Raymonde Chouinard.

Josée
Chouinard.

Josée's father,
André Chouinard.

Josée's brother,
Eric Chouinard.

Josée's first skating photo, age 8.
Paul Roy Photographe ENR.

One of Josée's first competitions, age 9.

Josée on ice,
age 13.

Josée at age 17.
Tom Hayim

Josée and husband
Jean-Michel.

Josée with Laval
Skating Club friends,
Chantal Gagnon and
Martin Marceau.

Josée with Olympic silver medalist, Brian Orser, 1983.

Josée and Isabelle Brasseur, with trainer, Charles Poliquin at
the 1992 Winter Olympics.

Josée with coach Joanne Barbeau.

Josée receiving last minute advice from her coach, Louis Stong.

Stephan Potopnyk

An interview with CBC commentator Brian Williams.
Canadian Figure Skating Association and F. Scott Grant

Josée with Karen Preston, at the 1992 Nationals.
Kolette Myers

Josée proudly showing her gold medal at the 1993 Nationals.

Josée and Kurt Browning performing their Western number, 2001 Stars on Ice.
G. Lisa Herdman

Josée and Kurt Browning tossing the first pitch at a Toronto Blue Jays game.
G. Lisa Herdman

Scott Hamilton
says goodbye to
Josée during his
final tour. Stars on
Ice, 2001.
G. Lisa Herdman

Josée and Elvis
Stojko.
Stephan Potopnyk

Josée and
Celine Dion at
Olympic promo.
Tom Sandler Photography

Josée with
husband,
Jean Michel
and
Bryan Adams.

Josée and
singing
sensation
Christina
Aguilera.

Josée and
Kurt Browning
performing at a
Stars on Ice
event.

Josée with Elizabeth Manley and Mary Jane Stong.

The Photographic Edge

Josée at Disney's Epcot Centre, with cyclist Kurt Harnett and Mickey Mouse.

Josée's promo shot for Lubriderm.

Winning performance at the 2000 Sears Pro/Am in Hamilton, Ontario.

G. Lisa Herdman

A happy Josée at Skate Canada, 1991.

Kevin Kooy

Josée performing at the
1991 Nationals.

Josée in 'her'
American in Paris
costume at the
1995 Canadian
Professional
Championships.
Stephan Potopnyk

Josée in her favourite costume performing to Moon River. Canadian Professional Championships 1995.

Stephan Potopynk

Josée in her 1994 Olympic 'garden' costume.

Stephan Potopynk

Josée and Barbara Ann Scott at Canadian Skating Legends night. Air Canada Centre, March, 1999.

Stephan Potopynk

Josée during pre-Olympic promotion, 1994.

Josée and her mom, Raymonde Chouinard.

last. He saw the joy on my face when I skated. Because I was happy, he was happy. I am also quite certain that if he had lived and I reacted to the outcome of any competition with guilt or shame, he would not have allowed it to fester. Instead, he would have given me a strong lecture about what is really important in life.

I still talk to my dad. If I'm at an important competition, I will say a few words to him at the start of my program. And I always feel as if he is on the ice with me. If I get tired during the middle of my routine, I'll ask for his help, and then I will smile, because I can just hear him telling me to get my lazy butt moving and finish the program.

• • • • •

One of the biggest changes I had to adapt to in my life occurred in the summer of 1993. Although I had made a mark in Canada with my two national titles, I wasn't making the expected advancements at the international level. At my first World Championship competition in 1991, I had placed sixth. Supposedly, this was a remarkable achievement for a debut performance at a competition of this stature. People were excited and there was talk that I had the potential to be a World Champion. The following year I moved up one position to fifth and I looked forward to perhaps standing on the podium in 1993. Instead, I plummeted to ninth. With the 1994 Olympics less than a year away, and what I thought may be my last World Championships a month after, I knew I was running out of chances to succeed as an amateur at the international level.

I didn't know why I couldn't reach my goals. It certainly wasn't for lack of effort, because I worked hard and put everything I had into skating. It also wasn't for lack of support. Both the city of Laval and my home rink were behind me 100 percent and gave me endless encouragement. My mother was also there for me. I still lived at home and she catered to my every need. Even though I was 23 years old, Mom was doing my laundry and cooking my meals. She even washed the laces on my skates and polished the boots! While I had friends in university or holding down steady jobs, I was leading a very relaxed life outside of the rink.

There had been no need for me to take on a part-time job, since my father had left us financially stable. Although it had been tough in the beginning because of some bad investments (which I didn't know about until years later), my mother soon learned how to handle the money and became very adept at providing for us. We weren't rich, but we were comfortable. I also had financial assistance from various corporations to subsidize the costs of my skating. Even though my club charged me a minimal membership fee, and I only had to pay for ice time during the evening hours, there were many other expenses to be covered. The costs of coaching, summer training, costumes, and choreography run high for skaters competing at the international level,

and can quickly deplete a family's funds. There-
fore, corporate sponsorship is a mainstay of most
world-class skaters, and I was fortunate to have
GAM, Pert Plus, and Suzuki by 1992. Lubriderm,
Almay, and others would come later. In turn, I
acted as a spokesperson for the companies, doing
commercials or allowing them to use my name
or image in advertisements. Because I was still
amateur, I wasn't permitted to take money di-
rectly. Instead, any reimbursements would go into
a trust fund from which I would have to request
whatever amount I needed.

Perhaps I had it too easy, I thought. If I became
more independent and sacrificed some of my com-
forts, then maybe my commitment to skating
would be even stronger. After much soul-search-
ing, I decided to leave home. Now I just had to
figure out where to go.

Around this time, I was also facing a dilemma
with my coach. Joanne had married and because
of demands at home, she told me she wanted to
cut back on travel. She also became pregnant that
year and decided not to accompany me to any
international competitions, other than one week
at the Olympics. This created a definite problem
for me. Having missed most of the 1992 Olympics, I wanted to experience the 1994 Games from
start to finish. Because I would be training while
I was there, I believed it was necessary for Joanne
to be with me. We talked about it but couldn't
reach an agreement. Joanne wanted me to hire
another coach, who would be secondary to her.

While I would continue training with Joanne, the other coach could accompany me to competitions. However, I didn't think this would be a suitable arrangement. A coach's role at a major competition is too important to the skater, and I believed that I should be training with the same person who was going to take me to these events. I wanted it to be Joanne, but if that wasn't going to be possible, I would have to look elsewhere.

I was very familiar with Doug Leigh at the Mariposa Club in Barrie, Ontario. He coached Elvis Stojko, Brian Orser, and Stephen Cousins, and had helped me out many times in the past. Because we sometimes tend to get too comfortable with our own coaches, skaters will often go to someone else to get a fresh perspective. With Joanne's blessing, I already trained with Doug for a week every summer and for another week in the fall. In my search for a new coach, I naturally thought of him. If he agreed, I would move to Barrie for the 10 months preceding the Olympics, and begin training there.

With my decision made, I called Doug, who seemed as excited by the prospect as I was. When I informed Joanne, however, she wasn't happy and turned down my offer to be secondary coach. She told me that she would be my first coach or nothing. Since I had no other choice, I reluctantly let her go. It was such a shame. I had tremendous respect for Joanne. She had taught me so much, and although I tried to keep in touch with her afterwards, she wanted little to do with me. I believe she was feeling the same pain of separation that I was. Hurt as it did, I believed this move was necessary for my career. Joanne had her priorities, which I totally understood. But I also had mine. To this day, however, I wish she was still a part of my skating career.

A couple of years earlier, I had signed with IMG, an international sports agency located in Toronto. After conferring with them, the general plan had been for me to retire from the amateur ranks at the end of the 1994 season. Although there weren't numerous opportunities for a professional skater at that time, IMG owned "Stars on Ice." And since I had been performing with the tour for awhile, I knew my run with Stars would continue as a professional. When my agents learned of my plans to move from Montreal, they thought it would be better if I trained with Louis Stong at the Granite Club in Toronto, rather than with Doug. Louis worked with Sandra Bezic, another client of IMG, who also did the choreography for "Stars on Ice," and IMG believed this group of people would be good for my future professional career. There was another persuading factor behind their reasoning. Kurt Browning, who was also their client, had begun training with Louis the year before. Our agents believed that it would be beneficial to both of us to skate together and motivate each other in this important Olympic year.

It all made sense to me. However, I didn't know Louis and had never had more than a five-minute conversation with him. Furthermore, my heart was with Doug. I admired his coaching skills and believed he could instill the confidence in me that I would need to compete at the Olympics. I didn't know what to do. Finally, I made the decision based on my relationship with Kurt. He and I were already the best of friends and we skated in similar styles. It would definitely benefit both of us to train together. I cried when I called Doug with the news. However, he acted like the professional he is and told me he understood.

Once I had made the decision to move to Toronto, the person I was most concerned about was my mother. Since Dad's death, her life centred around me and my skating. Because my brother was very independent, he didn't seem to need her as much as I did. But Mom and I would talk skating around the clock, and she really had no other outside interests. She was also still keeping most of her problems to herself. For instance, we had no idea that for many years she had suffered with angina. We only discovered it in 1991, when she had triple bypass surgery, and I'm absolutely convinced she would have kept the operation from us if it had been at all possible.

When I told Mom that I was moving to Toronto, she was upset, but she realized how important the change was for my skating career. Knowing that I would only be away for 10 months helped to alleviate her sadness. Still, it was troublesome for her. She told me afterwards that she felt so empty without me in the house. Thinking about herself wasn't something she was used to doing.

It was much easier to tell Jean-Michel. He understood, because he was also training and trying to earn a spot on the Olympic team. This was the most meaningful year of our lives as far as our careers went, and he knew the move would be best for me. Leaving my mother, brother, boyfriend, coach, friends, and the people at my club was the hardest thing I have ever had to do. However, I was positive that my decision would give me the strength and focus I needed in order to succeed.

I stayed with friends for the first month I was in Toronto, and in August, I found a place of my own. It was a furnished basement apartment that was tiny and practically windowless. But it was all mine and I loved it. For the first time in my life, I had to take full responsibility for everything I did. If I didn't shop for the groceries, I didn't eat. And it didn't take me long to learn that if I left the apartment untidy in the morning, it didn't magically clean itself up during the day.

Then there was the mattress. Thin as a piece of cardboard, I'd have an ongoing struggle with it during the night and would awaken in the morning stiff and sore. It only grew worse with time and a week before I left for the Olympics, I could hardly walk. My physiotherapist urged me to move from the apartment, or at the very least, purchase another mattress, but I knew it wasn't responsible for my back pain. It was all the weights I'd lifted and the falls I'd sustained. I had no intention of leaving my little nest. Nor was I about to buy another mattress. My move was expensive enough and I was watching every dime I spent.

Living in Toronto was such a cultural shock. A city of predominately English-speaking people, it seemed so big and confusing. On my first day in town, my agent, Nathalie Cook, took me to a Suzuki dealership north of Toronto, where I was going to pick up a car they had agreed to loan me. From there, I was going to an early-afternoon appointment at the CBC studio for a costume fitting for Kurt's upcoming television special, "You Must Remember This." When I was presented with the keys to a car with a standard transmission, I whispered to Nathalie, "But I don't know how to drive it." She conferred with the dealer and came back to tell me that it was either this car or the bus; the dealer didn't have an automatic to loan me. After a 20-minute crash course, I pulled out of the lot with the dealer shaking his head. I'm certain he thought he'd never see that car again. Armed with a map and a prayer, I began to make my way into the city.

Stalling the car at every intersection, I crept down one of the busiest streets in Toronto. Other drivers passed me every few minutes and angrily blared their horns. I was just lucky that I didn't have to stop on a hill. Somehow, I found the building, received my fitting, and within a short time was back in the car. But getting home was a nightmare. I was utterly lost, and it took me over five hours! I never swear, but I made an exception that day.

The next morning, in my limited English, I tried to tell Kurt about my experience, and he practically fell on the floor in laughter. Kurt was used to my heavy French accent, and in the past, we had always communicated as best we could. He knew a little French, and I knew a little English, and despite our language barrier, we managed to become close friends.

Although I had been taught some English in school, I didn't make any attempt to speak the language until I was about 14 years old. Around that time, I was selected to attend the CFSA-sponsored national training camps, where for a couple of weeks in late August, inexperienced skaters trained alongside national and international champions. Because the classes were conducted in English, I realized I would have to make more of an effort to understand and speak the language. But it almost didn't happen.

At one of the training camps, I was on a bus with the other skaters. Michael Slipchuk, an up-and-coming singles skater, was telling jokes in English. Because I couldn't understand what he was saying, my bilingual friends acted as interpreters. Often the punchline was lost in the translation, and the story wouldn't seem all that funny to me. After hearing another joke of Michael's, I bravely added a line in French, which my friends thought was hysterical. Michael mistakenly believed we were laughing at him, and said if I couldn't speak English, I shouldn't speak at all. Even though I hadn't comprehended any of the

English conversations that day, somehow I understood that remark.

Because of Michael's comment, I immediately became resentful about having to speak English. Generalizing, I thought anglophones acted a little too superior about their language. It wasn't my fault that I was born to a French-speaking family. Besides, I was proud of my heritage. So I stubbornly refused to speak English. But after awhile, I realized I had no choice in the matter. If I wanted to learn anything more about skating, I would have to master the language. And even though Michael had made that remark (which he denies to this day), we eventually became good friends. When I met up with him or Kurt at Nationals, I wanted to talk to them, and would try very hard to communicate in their language. But it wasn't until after I moved to Toronto and was in an English-speaking environment that my language skills greatly improved.

This was indeed a time of change for me. And perhaps the biggest adjustment I had to make was training with a new coach. I had never worked with a man before, and it took awhile to get used to. Furthermore, Louis was quite a bit older than me. Because we didn't have much in common other than skating, our relationship both on and off the ice was strictly professional. I was also somewhat intimidated by Louis. He was well-known throughout the skating world and was held in high esteem by skaters, judges, and other coaches. On top of that, he made a formidable pair with his wife, Mary Jane, who often found music for the skaters and designed their costumes.

As we worked on my skating, costumes, and programs, I grew a little dissatisfied with my looks. I had vowed to make this a year of change, yet every time I looked in the mirror, the same old me stared back. I wanted a fresh appearance, and decided a new hair colour might be just what I needed. Cutting my hair was out of the question. I had done that a few years back in an attempt to look older, and the end result had been less than flattering. With the decision made, I went to the drugstore and picked out a lovely shade of auburn that was supposed to wash out after eight shampoos.

I couldn't wait to see the transformation. After carefully following the instructions on the box, I dried my hair in much anticipation. When I was finished, though, I couldn't believe my eyes. My blonde hair was now a fluorescent shade of raspberry. I'm not exaggerating. I looked like a punk rocker! I tried washing it out, but the more shampoo I applied, the brighter it became. When Jean-Michel saw me, he thought I was wearing a clown wig. That's how bad I looked.

The next day, I went to the rink and faced Louis. I was a little nervous about this meeting because I was scheduled to shoot a commercial for Lubriderm that was to be shown nationwide. This was supposed to be a year in which I heightened my profile, and I didn't think my coach or my sponsors would appreciate my new look. You can imagine Louis' reaction. He almost had a heart attack. I assured him the colour would wash out within a week, but as it became pinker with each passing day, he frantically summoned Mary Jane for help. We called a colour specialist, who had to bleach and re-dye my hair. However, even the experts couldn't revert it back to its natural colour. If you saw the Lubriderm commercial and wondered why my hair was slightly orange, now you know why.

Louis was a very good coach, but at this stage in my career, I really didn't need anyone teaching me how to jump or spin. What I did require was someone to assess my overall skating technique and how I was presenting myself on the ice. Louis was perfect for the job and instantly sized up what I was lacking. Indeed, his eye for determining what skaters need to get better was so good that he went on to work with Skate Canada in the development of young skaters. Louis, Mary Jane, and Sandra Bezic certainly polished my look that year and put together two very memorable programs. Kurt was also a big influence on me, and the time we spent training together was invaluable. It was such an excellent team that after I turned professional the following year, I decided to stay in Toronto. I continued to work with Louis until 1996, when, after a disappointing year, we both decided to go our separate ways.

I never returned to Quebec to live on a full-time basis, which was hard on my mother in the beginning. However, she soon began to make a life of her own. Recently she turned our family home over to my brother and purchased a condominium for herself. And even though I am in Toronto and she is in Montreal, we see each other often and talk on the phone almost daily.

Experiencing independence that year was like a breath of fresh air to me. For the first time in my life, I was self-sufficient and in charge of my own destiny. And I liked the feeling. When I decided to move to Toronto, I made those changes in my life happen. Although it was scary to venture into the unknown, I grew and developed as a person in ways that I never dreamed possible. I'm not afraid to take chances now and I like the person I've become. And as far as change goes, I say, bring it on! It can only make you stronger.

CHAPTER SIX

Being Your Own Best Friend

I don't believe there is another sport that is as hard on women as figure skating. We are expected to perform difficult athletic moves with grace and beauty, and are judged as much by how we look as by what we accomplish on the ice. An unflattering hairstyle, too much or too little makeup, an inappropriate costume, or a couple of extra pounds can lower a judge's opinion and be reflected in our marks. It may not be fair, but it's the truth. And to survive in this image-driven sport, we need high self-esteem and confidence. Without them, we'd be lost.

No one knows this better than me. Spending much of my career absorbed in self-doubt and uncertainty about my body size, I realize now what a total waste of energy it was. However, feelings of insecurity are extremely common among female figure skaters, and I'd be willing to bet there isn't one of us who hasn't spent some time worrying about whether she is too fat, too short, too plain ... I could go on and on. I was lucky that my lack of confidence only showed up in an occasional shaky performance on the ice. When I wasn't feeling good about my physical appearance, I fretted over what the audience, judges, or other skaters were thinking. The worry was distracting and could result in a less-than-stellar performance. I've seen others, however, whose low self-esteem led to terrible eating disorders and mental problems. In a few cases, obsessions over body image have even resulted in abrupt endings to promising careers.

My own concerns with self-image began when I was 14 years old. It was a month before the sectional competitions, and I was in heavy training. Learning the double Axel, triple Salchow, and triple toe that summer, I wanted to show the judges what I could do and decided to include all three jumps in my program. Because the jumps weren't yet consistent, I repeatedly fell while practicing them. The more I went down, the more upset I became, which only made me more determined to include the jumps. At that point, I should have chosen just one and perfected it, but I stubbornly pushed on, and in the process I injured my back. Although I didn't know it at the time, the constant rotations of the attempted triples and the shock of falling on the ice had caused a disc to slip in my vertebrae.

Experiencing pain while I was training wasn't new to me, and I continued to skate. But within a short time, I was barely able to lift my arms. Excruciating muscle spasms were tearing at my back, making it difficult to breathe. Concerned, my coach told me that if I wanted to compete, I would have to rest for a few days.

The sectional competition was very important to me that year. For the first time, I had an excellent chance of winning and making myself known at the provincial level. Assuring my mother and coach that I was sufficiently recovered, I departed with them for the competition in high spirits. Being off the ice had done me good, and in the figures segment of the competition, I placed third. On the morning of the practice for the short program, however, the pain returned with a vengeance, and I limped off the ice in tears.

If I had been in a position lower than third, my coach would have pulled me out of the competition right then and there. But I had a shot at winning. While the two skaters ahead of me excelled in figures, I was stronger in style. If I skated well, the gold medal was mine. But first I needed treatment for the pain.

A friend of the family recommended someone in the area who was supposed to have the ability to heal with his hands. Although my mother was skeptical, she took me to see the person, who practiced out of his house. We should have realized something was amiss as soon as we stepped in the door. It was the middle of winter and there was no heat in the house. It was so cold that my mother kept her fur coat on while she waited. Meanwhile, I was led away to another room by a very old man. He asked me to remove my coat and sit down on a bench. Then he proceeded to pull on one of my feet, tugging so hard that I thought my leg would be left permanently longer than the other one. When he was finished, he took my shoulders in his hands and, without warning, cracked my back. I can't tell you how painful it was! Tears came to my eyes as my back throbbed in agony. Hearing the sound of my vertebrae cracking, my mother had come rushing into the room. I had never seen her sweat, but she was in such a panic that despite the cold, she removed her coat, unbuttoned her vest, and was wiping the perspiration from her forehead. Before she could open her mouth to speak, the old man twisted me to the other side, and again, we heard the sickening noise of crunching bone. It hurts me now just thinking about it.

Leaning on my mother while we walked to the car, I wondered how on earth I would be able to skate in 24 hours. The so-called healer assured us the pain was normal, but said I should apply ice and rest for three days. Returning to the hotel, I eased myself down on the bed while my mother held ice on my aching back. She wanted me to withdraw from the competition, but I blocked my ears to her pleas. Nothing was going to stop me from competing. After a restless night, I was back at the arena first thing in the morning for practice.

With my coach watching from the boards, I attempted all my jumps, but wasn't able to manage the triples. I was trying to hide how much pain I was in, but Joanne had only to look at my face. Grimacing and blinking back the tears, I again attempted a triple jump. By now, people in the stands were staring in shock at my mother, who meekly told them that she wasn't forcing me to skate. And it's true. It was all me. I just wanted to compete so badly. Joanne couldn't stand to see what I was doing to myself and ordered me off the ice. Forming words of protest, I hesitated, but knew it was all over when she walked away.

As soon as I arrived home, I saw a doctor in Montreal, who told me it would take four to six months before my back would be fully healed. Skating, or any other form of exercise, was banned from my routine. I was also advised not to walk, or even sit, for extended periods. According to the specialist, complete bed rest was the only solution. The diagnosis came in December, and although I began to skate a little in April, I wasn't back into my normal routine until June.

As a teenager, I weighed about 100 pounds before injuring my back. But during this time of inactivity, and because I was also going through puberty, I put on an additional 15 pounds. This may not sound like much to the average person, but with my 5'2" frame, the extra weight was very noticeable and would definitely hinder my ability to jump when I returned to the ice.

While I was recovering, there was very little to do other than watch television or read books. Within a few days, I had gone from someone who was always moving and busy to a stationary couch potato. I was so bored that the highlight of my day was thinking about what I was going to eat next. I have always loved food, but never had to worry about calories since I burned them off so quickly. Now, as I lay flat on my back flipping channels and munching on cookies, food became the centre of my universe. I ate non-stop. To make matters worse, my mother went away for a two-week vacation and hired a lady to stay with us who happened to be a wonderful cook. Desserts hadn't been part of my family's dinner routine, but now I looked forward to the end of the meal and the different sweet concoctions she prepared nightly. As I gulped down every last morsel of cake, ice cream, or pudding, I didn't give a thought to the tiny skating outfits that I would have to eventually squeeze myself into.

I grew so big that my own mother didn't recognize me when she returned from her trip. By then I was able to walk, and thought I would go to the airport to surprise her. She stared at me for a full 30 seconds before knowing who I was. "My goodness," she gasped. "What happened to you?" When she gently explained why she hadn't recognized me, I burst into tears. It had been a grand two weeks, but we both knew I had some serious work ahead of me if I had any intention of skating the following season.

I've never been a big believer in diets. My opinion is that if you eat sensibly and stay active, your body will usually reach and maintain its ideal weight. Everyone is different, however, and at times there may be medical reasons for a weight gain or loss. You should, of course, see a doctor if there is a concern. In my case, the reasons for the weight gain were obvious, and the first thing I did was cut back on my portions of food. I also restricted myself to healthy eating, which meant no more desserts or junk-food snacking. Then I started a training program. Because I needed to strengthen my back, my physiotherapist and doctor recommended abdominal exercises, and for overall toning and weight loss, I swam and cycled.

A couple of months ahead of schedule, my back felt good and I believed I was ready to return to the ice. Although my mother cautioned me, she didn't interfere with my plans. Mom was aware that skating had gone far beyond a recreational sport for me. She also realized how determined I was to succeed. Selections for the national training camp would be made in the summer and if I had any hope of being chosen, I would have to start skating soon. But the first few times I tried, I came home in tears. Unable to perform the simplest of moves without experiencing pain, I had to get off the ice. I was able to walk and exercise, but I still wasn't strong enough to skate. It was a very frustrating time. I'd return home from the rink silent and moody after another unsuccessful attempt. Without speaking a word to my mother, I'd go downstairs, turn up the volume on my stereo and perform sit-ups until my stomach muscles ached. I was probably hurting myself in the process, but it was my way of trying to get through the emotional and physical pain.

By the beginning of the summer, I was finally back on the ice. Since I hadn't jumped in six months, I had to start with the basics and relearn the jumps that had been the cause of my back injury the season before. Although I was still a few pounds overweight, I wasn't too troubled about the way I looked. I didn't even have to buy new skating outfits. Because they stretched, the practice clothes were very forgiving as they expanded a couple of sizes. Besides, by the middle of the summer I was training 10 hours a day at a skating school in Montreal. Between stroking, spinning, and jumping on the ice, and push-ups, ballet, karate, and other forms of conditioning exercises off the ice, I was certain I would be back to my ideal skating weight before long.

Because the summer school trained the elite of the Quebec skaters, it was here that Skate Canada picked skaters from our province to attend the national training camp. Representatives from the organization would travel from centre to centre across Canada to make selections at the novice, junior, and senior levels. I had been chosen in novice the year before, and because I had relearned my double Axel, triple Salchow, and triple toe, I was fairly certain that I would qualify again. I was excited to learn that I was indeed selected, but my bubble quickly burst when I heard there was a condition attached. Before arriving at camp, I had to lose five pounds. I was mortified. There

is no way you can tell a 14-year-old girl to lose
weight without her thinking she is fat. And in
my imagination, I wasn't just five pounds overweight – I was huge! That's when I realized that
my sport wasn't just about skating. It was also
about how I looked.

Overnight, I began to compare myself with other
girls. One of my best friends at the rink was very
skinny, and standing beside her, I felt so big. I
also became aware that other people were talking
about me. The previous summer, I had arrived at
the skating school very thin, having just recovered from mononucleosis. Now, I was tugging on
my skating outfits in an attempt to hide my
thighs, and I heard that some people were questioning whether I could come back and compete.
My reaction was to train even harder. I also ate
less, and for a few days before the weigh-in, I
restricted my intake to granola bars and plenty of
fruit and water.

I lost the weight before the start of training
camp, but I couldn't shake the feeling that I was
bigger than the other girls. When I started school
that autumn, I began to feel uncomfortable eating my lunch around other people. To me, they
were thinner than I was, and I felt self-conscious
putting anything into my mouth for fear of what
they thought. I'd bring my lunch home untouched,
and Mom would ask me why I hadn't eaten.
Thank goodness I could talk to her and my coach.
I'd pour out my self-doubts, and between the two
of them, they didn't allow my worries to get out

of control. But if I hadn't have taken the advice of such good people around me, my situation could have become much worse and even dangerous.

When I was a teenager, I was vaguely aware that some girls and women experienced eating disorders, but it was not something I saw first-hand or discussed with my circle of friends. At that age, I don't think I fully understood that, in an effort to lose weight, some people would binge and then make themselves vomit, or take laxatives or diet pills in order to get rid of the food. I'm glad it was something I wasn't introduced to. Like most teenagers, I was very impressionable. I like to think that even without the supportive people around me, I would never have gone down that path. But who knows? The intense pressure to be thin in this sport can be overwhelming, and it can have the power to take over your sensibilities.

As I became older and more knowledgeable about eating disorders, I saw the dreadful toll they took on people around me, and I had no desire to be a part of it. Yes, I worried about how I looked on the ice, but I didn't resort to these drastic measures in order to lose weight. Anorexia or bulimia may begin as a way to drop a few pounds, but the disorders quickly get out of hand and can ruin a person's life.

I've observed many skaters on tour and at competitions who have eating disorders, and it's very disheartening to see. Often, these women will skate with a confidence that belies their total lack of self-esteem. They don't have to be themselves on the ice as they escape into the characters they're portraying, but immediately after they take their bows, their low self-image returns. I know one skater who was an amazing performer and delighted audiences with her gutsy style. She was also bulimic. When she stepped out of the spotlight she didn't like who she was, and admitted that performing was the only time she felt good about herself. Obsessing over the way she looked, her hair, makeup, clothes, and body size had to be perfect. I watched her grow thinner and thinner over the years as she threw up the little food she consumed. Her increasingly pale skin took on a bluish tinge as the veins appeared close to the surface because her blood wasn't circulating properly. It was so sad. She was a kind and generous person who didn't know how beautiful she was on the inside.

I have also seen some skaters come off the ice with broken bones because they are so frail from a lack of nutrition. Because they're missing important vitamins and minerals from their bodies, a fall or a wrong turn that would never injure a healthy athlete causes fractures and breaks. I can remember one pairs skater who was so weak after her program that her partner had to carry her off the ice. She hadn't eaten properly in months.

I don't want to frighten anyone from getting into skating. It's true that as triple jumps become mandatory among female skaters, the need to be lighter and smaller has escalated. As a result, eating disorders are probably more apparent. But this goes far beyond figure skating. In today's age, it seems that women in general are obsessing more than ever about their looks and body size. It doesn't matter if we are executives, homemakers, students, or figure skaters. As we see rail-thin models staring back at us from the magazine pages and fashion runways, we are led to believe that thin is beautiful. We have to change this misconception, because it's a ridiculous notion. But it seems we're never satisfied with who we are. I've had women approach me and say they would love to be as small as I am. Well, let me tell you something. If I had a choice when the size genes were being handed out, I'd be around 5'8" with legs that went on forever! Since I know that's not going to happen in this lifetime, I've learned to like what I have been given.

Don't let anyone else, other than a doctor, tell you how much you should or shouldn't weigh. There was a time when coaches regularly put their skaters on the scales and berated them if they were even a pound overweight. None of my coaches ever criticized me about the way I looked, and I was blessed in that respect. I've heard and seen some coaches who were very hard on their female skaters. Today, their words and actions would be considered abusive and would not tolerated by educated skaters or their parents.

There is nothing wrong with wanting to improve your looks, as long as it doesn't become an obsession or a top priority. You should want to be the best person you can be on the inside as well as the outside. That means leading a healthy and positive lifestyle. Eat properly and don't deprive yourself. If you're working out, make sure you are training for the right reasons. Don't do it to fit into a smaller dress size or to try to look like someone else. Do it for yourself, because it makes you feel good.

Over the last few years, I have become very confident about who I am. Of course, some of my self-assurance has developed naturally with maturity. But for the most part, I've had to work at it. When I lost the national title in 1996, I don't believe I have ever felt so terrible about myself. It took everything I had to pull out of the depression I'd fallen into, and I will tell you more about that in a later chapter. Eventually, however, I learned that I was my own worst enemy. And aren't we all? We put ourselves down in ways that we would never think of doing to anyone else. I try now to accept and like myself exactly as I am down to every last imperfection, and I urge you to do the same. There is nothing nicer than becoming your own best friend.

CHAPTER SEVEN

Think Like
A Champion

When I was young, I skated for the sheer pleasure
of the sport and never dreamed about becoming a
World or Olympic Champion. I watched the international competitions on television and admired the skaters, but I just couldn't see myself
at that level. Even when I got older and was told I
had the potential to reach the Olympics, I couldn't
imagine myself on the podium. In my mind, those
three positions were reserved for other skaters.

When I won my first national title in 1991 and
came sixth at Worlds a couple of months later,
people said I had the "complete package." This
meant I possessed the technical and artistic talent to compete against the best in the world. I
know now, however, that I was lacking in one
important area: the ability to realize that I de-
served to be there. Olympic gold medal winners
Kristi Yamaguchi and Tara Lipinski say they as-
pired to be Olympic Champions from the time
they were five years old. The seed was planted in
their minds at an early age, and they worked to-

wards achievement of this ultimate goal. They saw themselves as Olympic Champions and they became what they thought about.

My goals were not so lofty. I worked from one competition to the next and successfully accomplished what I set out to do. As I rose higher through the ranks in Canada, winning the National Championships became my ambition. I could see myself holding the Canadian title and went on to actualize this dream three times over. But it stopped there. Physically, I was capable of claiming a World or even an Olympic medal. It was the mental aspect that held me back in my amateur career. Deep down, I probably believed I wasn't good enough.

Since turning professional, and with my newfound confidence, I have changed my mindset 100 percent. I now presume that no matter who I'm competing against, or how high-profile the event is, I am as deserving as the next person to win. When I came first at the Sears Pro-Am in 2000, I'm certain many believed that I wouldn't be able to go up against Michelle Kwan, the undisputed queen of the amateur skating world. However, I believed I could. I knew I had the jumps, the artistry, and the technical skills. I never let my confidence waver and I won the competition. And it didn't happen because the others gave a poor performance. In fact, everyone skated brilliantly. I'm proud of this accomplishment because it shows who I've become. It also proves something that I wish I had practiced on a routine basis years ago: to become a champion, one must think like a champion.

Before you ever step onto the ice to compete, you must believe in yourself. Never tell yourself ahead of time that it is okay to be third or thirteenth. Go to the competition with the intention of winning. Aim for the top of the podium. If you participate in an event without a strong belief in yourself, it will definitely be reflected on the ice. Obviously, you're not going to win a medal at every competition, and at times, you may even place far below your expectations. There will be disappointments in your skating career, as there will be in your everyday life. It's how you handle them that matters. With a positive and upbeat attitude, you'll learn from your mistakes and strive to do better at the next event.

When you feel strong and in charge, you will be taking control of your environment. This is a key step towards maintaining confidence. I'm not saying that you should be cocky or arrogant – those types of people tend to irritate others and alienate themselves – but you should always try to be in control of yourself and your surroundings. As I've mentioned in earlier chapters, you can use visualization ahead of time to ensure that you will be in control. This way, there will be no surprises, since you have already lived the event from start to finish in your mind.

When I arrive at a rink for a competition, I take control of my environment as soon as I step through the door. Self-assured because I'm prepared, I know who my competitors are and am familiar with their pre-competition habits. I'm aware of who likes to arrive early and who prefers to come later. I know where the various coaches or team leaders will be standing or sitting in the arena. Because I've already been through it all in my mind, I'm very comfortable. I take charge of my surroundings and I don't let anyone else affect my mood or positive thoughts. If I want to talk, I will initiate the conversation in the dressing room. But if I feel that I need to detach myself from what is going on around me, I will politely refrain from dialogue. No competition is identical, and different situations call for different reactions. Either way, I've thought it out ahead of time and know what my game plan will be depending on the circumstance. I don't deviate from the plan and I don't give up my control or composure.

Taking control of your environment can be applied outside of the rink as well. For example, experienced public speakers use this method when talking to large audiences. They practice their speeches out loud and visualize an audience in front of them. Then, when they actually give the speech, they are relaxed and in full control because they're just repeating the performance they already gave in their minds. The unexpected may happen, but it won't ruffle their performance. By preparing yourself ahead of time, you will be able to take charge of any situation in which you may have otherwise felt uncomfortable. It's a terrific confidence booster because when you feel good about what's going on around you, you feel good about yourself.

One of the best ways to prepare yourself for a competition is by using a 21-day plan. The theory is that, three weeks prior to an event, you should be the person you want to be, both mentally and physically. There should be no changes to your program. Your training should be down cold – meaning you should practice the same elements in the same order every day. And your visualization process should be almost perfect. Practice your routines both mentally and physically for 21 days, and unless there are some unforeseen circumstances, your actual performance should follow very close to what you planned.

I learned this technique from a man named Lucien Roy, who was doing research on accelerated learning when I was younger. Along with Stephan Eivars, another skater at the club, who also happened to be my boyfriend at the time, I was chosen to work with Lucien as he conducted his experiments. Believing that it takes three weeks to make or break a habit, Lucien taught me how to accomplish a major goal in 21 days. For instance, in 1992, I decided I wanted to learn the triple Axel. Lucien created a tape of me performing a double Axel, and graphically added another rotation to it. If you viewed the tape, it looked like I was actually performing a triple. I watched the tape morning and night for 21 days, and after awhile, my brain was tricked into believing that I could perform a triple Axel. During this period, I didn't attempt the jump on the ice, although I did practice my double Axel every day. After three weeks, I stepped onto the ice believing I knew how to do the jump. And in my first attempt, I landed the triple Axel. It was truly amazing!

Back then, most women weren't including this jump in their repertoires. It was difficult to learn and too risky to perform in competition. Because the jump wasn't necessary, I stopped practicing it on a regular basis. Eventually, I lost the ability to land the triple Axel. A couple of years ago, however, I rediscovered this challenging jump. It was during the summer, when I wasn't feeling very motivated to train. Because I don't hold an Olympic or World title, offers to skate in competitions and events are occasionally hard to come by. If I didn't have anything scheduled, I reasoned, why bother to train at all?

By then, I was at the Mariposa Club with Doug Leigh, who couldn't help but notice my lacklustre mood. Doug suggested I relearn the triple Axel. At first I was skeptical. No Canadian woman has ever landed a triple Axel in competition, and at that stage in my career, I didn't think it was likely that I would be the first. However, I soon warmed to the idea. Attempting the triple Axel would motivate me to train by giving me a goal. So for a three-week period beforehand, I practiced the jump over and over in my head, while practicing my double Axel on the ice. And guess what? On or around the 21st day, I landed the triple Axel.

I still haven't attempted the jump in competition, although I do practice it on a fairly routine basis. Most of the competitions a professional skater enters are by invitation only, and if I'm lucky, I am asked to compete twice a year. (Don't ask me why, because I think I've more than proven myself.) If I was doing four or five competitions a season, I wouldn't hesitate to include the triple Axel in one of my programs. But because there is such a great length of time between the competitions I am invited to, attempting this difficult jump would be too chancy.

Lucien Roy taught me so much. Every week, he would visit Stephan and me to instruct us in whatever area he was testing. A busy man, he worked with both skaters and executives of large corporations. But he was passionate about skating. He had two daughters in the sport and was also a judge. In addition to teaching us the 21-day plan, Lucien helped us with our off-ice workouts by preparing tapes of the various exercises he thought we should do, which motivated me to keep up with this important area of training. Before Lucien, I would start an off-ice routine, become bored, and abandon it after a couple of weeks. Teaching us about imagery, visualization, and positive thinking, Lucien proved to Stephan and me that if we could see the results in our minds beforehand, we could make it happen.

I was 17 when I began training my brain as much as my body. But after a few years, I stopped practicing it so intensely because I was actually scaring myself. Knowing that my physical state would follow whatever my thoughts had been – either good or bad – almost became a burden. Lucien had warned me this could happen. I took it all very seriously and he saw that I was thinking way too much. Instead of using this strong tool in the way it was meant to be used, I started analyzing every thought and where it would lead me. It was mentally exhausting and tired me more than any physical workout could.

Eventually, the psychological fatigue showed up in my skating. Although I was executing all the elements in a nearly flawless manner, I was so drained from preparing every last detail in my mind that I was skating with very little feeling. I was almost like a robot. Performing in this style didn't score me any points with the judges, either. Two routines can be technically equal, but the one that is skated with the most heart will always win out. Over time, I learned that the secret is balance. We must prepare ourselves, but not be so preoccupied with, and worried about the future that we fail to live in the moment.

• • • • •

At some point in every novice skater's career, he or she is going to enter a competition and be overwhelmed with awe while practicing and performing alongside the more experienced skaters. If you find yourself in this situation, try to keep these feelings under control by remembering that these skaters were once in the same position as you. We all have to begin somewhere. Just keep in mind that every competition is new and is open for anyone to win. Furthermore, competition at any level isn't easy. Just showing up and trying your best is a brave endeavour in itself. Be proud that you've found the courage to come this far.

Many times, I've seen inexperienced skaters suffer from a defeatist attitude. They see the talent they have to go up against and give up before they begin to skate. If you think you're going to come in last before you even step onto the ice, chances are you won't be standing anywhere near the podium when the competition is finished. As insecure as I may have been at times about the way I was skating, I never went to a competition believing that everyone else was going to beat me. I do remember one event, however, in which I was in such absolute awe of the other skaters that my coach had to pull me off the ice.

It was at my first senior Worlds in 1991 and I had never seen so much skating talent under one roof. I had been to sectional and divisional competitions where some of the other skaters had impressed me, and when I reached Nationals, there were several who were at the top of their game. But I always took it in stride and concentrated on what I had to do. At this Worlds, though, I was stunned at the calibre of skating around me. Instead of practicing, I just stood in the middle of the ice and watched the more experienced women as they spiralled, spun, and jumped. Although I had seen some of these great athletes on television, to be standing on the same ice with them was a whole other story. I held them in such admiration that I didn't know where to look next.

My coach finally told me to get off the ice because she didn't want the other skaters to see how struck I was by them. She was right. I would have to compete against these women in a couple of days, and my gawking would have given them even more confidence and, perhaps, an edge over me. She suggested we sit in the stands and observe the other skaters from there. "You'll get it out of your system," she said, "and at the next practice, they'll be watching you." It was good advice. The following day, I was practicing alongside them as if I'd been doing it for years. I didn't feel intimidated or out of place, and I ultimately beat some of the women I had so admired on my first day of practice.

Although my placement at those Worlds was considered high for a newcomer, I believe I could have done even better. But I think I was unconsciously putting limits on myself. When I claimed my first National title earlier that year, it was difficult for me to accept the changes that occurred in my life. Overnight, I was the Canadian Champion, and I had a hard time dealing with the attention it brought to me. No longer was I the little girl from Laval, Quebec, who skated because she loved the sport. I was treated differently and people suddenly expected great things from me. In hindsight, I believe that not only did

I doubt that I had what it took to become a World Champion, but I wondered if I could accept the responsibilities and fame that came with the title. I feared more change and didn't know if I could handle it. Being the Canadian Champion was enough for me, and I presumed that I had reached my pinnacle.

I am telling you this now because I want you to know how imperative our thinking and belief systems are. Thoughts are powerful and can take us to the most joyous of places. They can also destroy us. Because of my thoughts, I was sabotaging any chances I had at a World title and unknowingly jeopardizing my advancement on the international scene. Don't get me wrong. I wanted to win, but the belief in myself just wasn't there. I would train hard and skate well through the qualification round and the short program. But after positioning myself for a medal by placing third or fourth, I would lower my level of performance down a notch, unconsciously ensuring that I wouldn't win a medal.

The most glaring example I can offer of how I undermined my talent happened at the 1994 World Championships. After my disappointing show at the Olympics (which I told you about in Chapter One and which is a perfect example of someone not taking control of his or her environment), I was very upset with myself and believed my career might be over. We had no idea then of the way figure skating would become such a popular sport with the public, and since I was supposed to retire after the Games, my life as a professional skater looked bleak. I didn't have a World or Olympic title, so I assumed it was all over for me.

The World Championships were less than three weeks away, however, and I knew that if I skated well, a medal would be there for the asking. Being in one of the top three positions would redeem me and perhaps give me a better chance at a professional career. But I didn't allow it to happen. My first mistake occurred during the qualification round. I was skating beautifully, and near the end of my program it dawned on me that if I skated perfectly, I may not be able to repeat my good performance when it counted. My last jump was supposed to be a triple toe, which is an easy jump for me, but because I was worried about a program that was a couple of days away, I doubled the jump. It was as if I was thinking I had to keep the best for the final. Although I won the qualification round even with the double toe, completing the jumps as I originally planned may have bolstered my confidence. Never save your best for some other day.

In the short program, I was determined to take control of the ice. I had a little wobble on my flying sit spin, but skated the rest of the performance according to plan and came third behind Surya Bonaly and Yuka Sato. Because I had beaten both women in other competitions, people were saying that I had a very good chance at winning the long program, which would have given me the title. I had also been skating beyond belief at practice. Kurt had retired after the Olympics and was at Worlds commentating for television. He remarked several times on how well I was skating.

Just after my name was announced for the long program, a disturbing and unwelcome thought popped into my head. What if I missed my first couple of jumps? Then, without wanting to, I saw myself falling on them and the vision filled me with fear. It was almost like another person had taken over my brain and I couldn't control my thoughts. Then I made a terrible mistake. Instead of going to my coach and telling him that I was suddenly overwhelmed with negative thoughts, I stepped onto the ice, skated to the centre, and proceeded to give the title away.

It wasn't like I did it on purpose. I wanted to win, and when it came time to making that first jump, I must have leapt six feet into the air in an attempt to overrule the self-defeating thoughts that had taken over my brain. But I fell to the ice on the triple flip. Then I did it again on the Lutz. I had gone out there and reenacted what I had thought about moments before. As a consequence, I came fifth at a World Championship competition that I should have won.

If I had only taken the time to talk to my coach beforehand. You're always allowed a couple of minutes after your name is called before you have to appear on the ice. Often, skaters use that time to collect their thoughts and refocus if necessary. Louis may have been able to help me. Experts say

121

it takes 10 positive thoughts to erase one negative thought, and my coach would have given me
the reinforcement I needed to get back on track.
But I didn't have the nerve to tell him, too em-
barrassed to confess what had been going through
my head. I didn't want to admit it to myself, let
alone my coach.

Afterwards, I was more ashamed of myself for
having those thoughts and not doing anything
about them than I was by how I skated. It actually took me two years before I acknowledged it,
and even more time before I was comfortable talking about it. I wonder now why I was so humili-
ated by my thoughts, as I'm certain many people
must have similar experiences before an important or stressful event – moments of self-doubt,
fear, and wondering, "what if?" I had trained all
my life for this moment and instead of grabbing
the brass ring, which was right at my fingertips, I
let it all go. I made certain that I wouldn't win.
And I was sure that if I told people, they would
think I was crazy.

I could probably analyze what happened to me
forever, but the bottom line is that we truly become what we think about. Today I know what
I'm worth and I focus on my strengths. When I
have a problem, I talk about it and try to resolve
it as soon as possible. I believe in myself and
what I can do both on and off the ice. If I had
followed this during the later stages of my amateur years, my life would be very different today.

Not that I'm complaining. I'm very grateful for what I have and there is little I would change.

I hope I've shown you how important it is to think like a champion in your skating career or in anything else you want to do with your life. Skaters like Scott Hamilton, Michelle Kwan, Kurt Browning, and Katarina Witt exude confidence and grace in their skating performances and in their personal lives. These qualities are part of their personalities. It's true that they all hold Olympic or World titles, and some would argue that they act like champions because they are champions. But I knew Kurt long before he won the first of his four World titles, and he was exactly the same then as he is now. He has always thought like a champion. And so can you.

CHAPTER EIGHT

Fight Through the Blues

At the end of the 1994 competitive season, I felt so empty inside. I had given everything to my sport for the year preceding the Olympics, and now I had nothing left to give. My body and mind were drained of all energy, and on the airplane home from Japan, where the World Championships had been, I wondered how I was going to face my future commitments. More than anything, I just wanted to crawl into bed, pull the covers up around me, and make the world go away.

Because there's a 14-hour time difference between Japan and Toronto, it usually takes me about three weeks before I feel like I'm back to normal. But after this trip, there was no time to rejuvenate my body or my spirit. Rehearsals for "Stars on Ice" were scheduled to start within a week and I had two new programs to prepare before joining the rest of the cast in Halifax. When Stars was finished touring the country, I was going straight to Victoria, where rehearsals would begin for "Skate the Nation," another cross-country tour. Overwhelmed with fatigue and sadness, I became exhausted even thinking about it. Furthermore, I was so ashamed of myself that I didn't want to face anyone when I got home. I was especially worried about what my fellow skaters would think of me.

When I finally arrived in Halifax, my head was in a fog. We have an expression in French – "dans la lune," loosely translated as "on the moon." It's used to describe a person who may be physically present, but his or her mind is somewhere else in the universe. And that's exactly how I felt – like I was on another planet. Because I was tired and unhappy, I had a difficult time learning the steps to the group numbers. And seeing the other skaters hurt even more than I thought it would. Their condolences were meant to comfort me, but I wasn't ready to hear or talk about what happened. To top it off, I was having trouble with my skates. And because I had lost all faith in myself, I wondered if the problem with my skating was because of my blades and boots, or perhaps it was just me. Maybe I couldn't do it anymore, I thought, and I tore myself apart with blame and criticism.

Things went from bad to worse on the tour. My feet didn't feel like they were a part of me and I couldn't seem to control what they did. Instead of gliding across the ice, I actually felt like I was skating a few inches above the surface. My blades would touch each other and I'd stumble on the easiest of transition movements. I stepped out of almost every jump because I was too afraid to follow through.

I honestly believe that I came to hate myself during this period. I rarely smiled either on or off the ice, and later heard that people were having a hard time approaching me. I was probably repelling them through my facial expressions and body language because I was certain that everyone was looking at me and thinking about my performance at Worlds. Talk about being paranoid! People may have watched, and some of them may have even been a little concerned, but I'm sure most of them forgot about it soon after. I was the one stuck in the time warp. I couldn't move past the day of my long program at the World Championships.

Eventually I spoke to a sports physiologist, who helped me somewhat. But I didn't talk to any of the other skaters because I didn't want to remind them of the way I had skated. I realize now how silly I was being. Here I was touring with a group of other people who all had endured similar experiences at one point or another during their careers. If I had confided in any of them, I'm positive they would have shown me they couldn't have cared less how I skated at Worlds, and that everyone wasn't focusing on my past performances. They had their own lives to worry about.

After "Skate the Nation" was over, I decided to take a month off and think about what I was going to do. Other than the time spent recuperating when I had injured my back, it was the first instance I had ever been away from the ice for such a long period, but I believed I needed to get some perspective on my skating career.

Earlier, the International Skating Union (ISU) had made a ruling that allowed professional skaters to reinstate as amateurs. Several of them had jumped at the chance and had competed at the last Olympics. Knowing the regulation would permit me to come back the following year if I wanted, I decided to retire from amateur competition in June. It would do me good to explore the different sides of skating. And if I could find the energy and the will, I would rejoin the amateur ranks for the 1996 World Championships, which were going to be held in Edmonton.

When I returned to the ice a month later, it was like a weight had been lifted from my shoulders. I skated and jumped with ease, and it was hard for me to believe that only a couple of months before, I was having such trouble. Offers to compete in professional competitions were also coming in at a surprising rate. I thought I might have blown my chances with the performances I gave at Olympics and Worlds, but I soon came to realize that people didn't think I had skated so badly. As usual, I had been my own harshest judge.

I loved skating at the professional events and competitions. Although I took them just as seriously as any amateur event, there was a show-business aspect that wasn't as evident in the ama-

teur world of skating. It was also inspiring to be
competing against women who I had long admired
from afar. I can recall being beside myself with
excitement when I showed up at one event and
saw Olympic silver medallist Rosalynn Sumners
in the dressing room. I told her that I had been a
fan for years, was looking forward to skating with
her, and that I particularly enjoyed a number she
did entitled "The Rose." In it, she wore a flowing
red dress and performed the most beautiful spiral
while holding a single red rose. It made quite an
impression on me and I never forgot it. Rosalynn
laughed when I expressed my enthusiasm about
skating with her. Funny, but she didn't think she
was all that special, and even revealed that "The
Rose" wasn't one of her favourite numbers. I
would remember that experience years later when
younger skaters came to me and told me that I
was their inspiration. We never see ourselves as
others see us.

I did well in my first year as a professional,
coming second at the North American Open and
then winning the Canadian Professional Championships. But more importantly, I rediscovered my
love for skating. I had pulled myself through that
difficult period after Worlds by changing my focus. And by the following spring, I was ready to
reinstate as an amateur.

We put together two new programs that I was
proud of and I worked hard to perfect my technical skills. I also believed my year as a professional paid off, as my artistry had never been bet-

ter. Come autumn, I participated in two international competitions, placing third at Skate Canada and then winning the Trophée de France.

In the past, I had always aimed to peak at Nationals, meaning that I would gear myself to be at the top of my game for this competition. But this particular season, Louis and I developed a different strategy, scheduling my training so that I would peak at the World Championships. Because I was skating so strongly, I truly believed I could win the coveted title. And this was my ultimate goal. Adding to my resolve was the desire to win Worlds in my home country. My mindset had never been so positive. No murky negative thoughts were going to stand in my way and pull it all out from under me again.

It was practically taken for granted that I would win Nationals. My competitors were younger and much less experienced than I was. And anyone who saw my programs said they were further advanced than the routines of the other skaters who would be participating at the Canadian Championships. It also didn't bother me that only one Canadian woman would be allowed to compete at Worlds as a result of the country's poor showing the year before. I believed, without a doubt, that the woman going to Worlds would be me. This belief did not come from arrogance or conceit. It was based on a firm consensus from those "in the know" that I was the most experienced skater and the most qualified to represent Canada at the World Championships.

Nationals were in Ottawa that year, and I arrived confident and eager to compete. On the first day of practice, however, I got the surprise of my life as I watched the other women skate. All of my main competitors seemed to be at their peak. They were executing triple jumps with looks on their faces that expressed their own determination to do well. Jennifer Robinson and Susan Humphreys, in particular, both seemed ready to fulfill dreams of their own. I began to worry, thinking that perhaps Louis and I had erred in our decision for me to peak at Worlds. The more I watched the other women, the more nervous I became.

I remember being at the rink, where I had just finished one of the worst practices of my life. I couldn't seem to do anything right. Voicing my concerns to Louis, I felt a panicky stirring inside. But my coach wasn't worried. Although he agreed that he'd never seen me skate so poorly, he believed it was good to get it all out of my system before the competition. He told me to forget about the ill-fated practice and move on. But I didn't. I carried it around with me and fretted even more. Instead of being relaxed, the way a skater of my experience should have been, I grew tense and stiff.

As my confidence about the way I was skating plummeted, so did my self-esteem about the way I looked. Suddenly, I felt fat. I can recall putting on one of my skating outfits, standing in front of the mirror, and staring at myself, wondering where the weight had come from. In reality, I wasn't overweight, but I was used to competing against people my own age or older. In Ottawa, I was going up against youngsters who were very thin and toned and I was subconsciously comparing myself to them. It was the last thing I needed.

The day before the competition, I was practicing on the ice and I fell. From the stands, I heard a group of children laughing. They had been allowed in the rink to watch the practice, and now they were snickering at me. Or so I thought. A million different things were running through my mind, and I didn't like the way I was feeling one little bit.

On the day of the short program, I didn't skate too badly, but I missed my combination jump and came second behind Jennifer. Going into the long program, I was so upset. But nobody else around me appeared to be concerned. I was in the dressing room with Mary Jane and I confided in her as to how I was feeling. She said, "I don't know why you're worrying. You are skating so well." I felt like screaming, "Hello! Doesn't anybody see what's going on here?" But there was no time to unravel the mess in my head, as we were being called to the ice for warm-up.

I was scheduled to skate first and I have always hated that position. I get so pumped up during the warm-up that I find the 30 seconds after we have cleared the ice, and before my name is called, is not enough time to bring me back down to the restful place I need to be in. When we were drawing for the skating positions earlier, I predicted that I was going to pick that spot. Everything else had gone wrong so far, and I figured it would just be my luck.

I stood with Louis at the boards and although I am certain my fear was apparent in my face, he didn't seem to be aware of how uncomfortable I was. For quite some time, we really hadn't been communicating. Louis had been considering taking a position with Skate Canada and for a month prior to Nationals, he wasn't at the rink very much. In fact, I believe I only saw him on one day for about 15 minutes. I want to make it clear that I'm not blaming Louis for what was about to happen. I was a big girl with years of experience under my belt, and I'm sure Louis thought I was on top of my training. And I was. In hindsight, however, my coach and I should have been closer prior to this important event.

As I waited for my music to begin, I remember trying to tune everything out, realizing that I must concentrate on each element as it came up. Although I doubled my first Salchow, I wasn't too disturbed because I knew I had many other triples in the program. But then I doubled my second jump. It was like an out-of-body experience. Because I hadn't managed any of the planned triple jumps, towards the end of my program I replaced the double Axel with a triple toe. I needed to add more triples to ensure a win, but I was running out of time. There was still a spin to perform, and before I knew it, the last strains of my music were playing. It was all over.

At times like this, I wish I was a better actor. Instead of bowing graciously with the smile of a champion, I communicated my disappointment in my performance to the audience and judges with my rounded shoulders and sad face. And I believe it affected my marks. It isn't over until it's over – and that is so true in skating. By acting confident afterwards, I would have been telling the judges to mark the overall package, because really, I didn't even have to jump in this competition. The other women, who would follow me, skated from element to element and many of them cheated on their jumps. There was also very little polish to their programs because they were so inexperienced. But through my body language, I told the judges that I didn't deserve the title.

After I finished skating, I went into a room backstage and fell to pieces. I was crying so hard that I couldn't stand up. Although Louis, Mary Jane, my mother, Jean-Michel, and others were trying to soothe me, I couldn't be consoled. There were still five other skaters who had yet to perform, and I can remember wishing they wouldn't skate well. I have never thought that before or since, but I was beside myself with pain. It wasn't so much that I feared losing the Canadian Championships, but it was knowing that only one woman would be allowed to go to Worlds. The reason I had reinstated was to get to that competition and prove that I could come through at the international level.

One by one, the other women skated, and I held onto my first-place position. But then Jennifer's turn came, and to give her credit, she saw her opportunity and went for it. In a judging split – with the one judge who went against me coming from Barrie, where Jennifer skated – I came second and my chance at getting to Worlds vanished into thin air. I would also be leaving amateur skating in the most horrible way I could imagine.

I completely broke apart when I heard the news, and I told Louis that I couldn't face going out to the podium for the medal ceremony. "Look at me," I cried. "How can I possibly present myself in this state?" I was numb with shock and couldn't feel my body. I could hardly walk. But of course, I had to go. Susan Humphreys, who came third, supported me as I made my way to the ice. She stood behind me and held me up, whispering that I was going to be okay. If I didn't say it then: thank you, Susan.

I have had low points in my life, but this was the absolute lowest. It sounds selfish of me to say, but at the time, the agony felt as bad as it did when I lost my dad. I wanted to run away and hide. I don't recollect standing on the podium. I've totally blocked it out, but I do remember feeling like I'd fallen down a very deep black hole.

• • • • •

Less than a week later, I had to get back on the ice because I was representing Canada at the

Grand Prix in France. There I was, up against seven of the most talented skaters in the world, including Michelle Kwan, Irina Slutskaya, and Lu Chen, who was the 1995 World Champion. And even feeling as miserable as I did, I came third. Being on the podium lifted my spirits, but not much. Although people kept telling me what a remarkable performance I had given, I wondered who would ever remember the results of a Grand Prix. And somehow it just didn't seem fair that all of these women, including those who didn't reach the podium, were heading to the World Championships without me. Their countries sent the best skaters, and they couldn't understand why I wasn't going to be competing. Neither did I.

I went to Worlds as a spectator, and only because Jean-Michel was competing. Poor guy. He had won Canadians and was probably having a hard time enjoying his victory with my depressing moodiness. He and his partner came seventh at Worlds, and of course I was happy for him. But to tell you the truth, it was awful being there.

From the end of the 1994 season until sometime in 1997, I felt like I was riding a roller coaster. I went up and down so many times that it was dizzying. But in the spring of 1996, I think I hit rock bottom, and I wondered if I would ever recover.

I came to "Stars on Ice" with an even worse opinion of myself than I had in 1994. I was nervous, with zero confidence. And because I was so uncomfortable with myself, I floundered on the ice. I couldn't seem to get my feet under me and even had trouble performing a double Axel. After awhile, I noticed a huge difference in the audience reaction to the way I was skating. Although the crowd would cheer loudly when my name was announced, they didn't clap as much after my performance as they normally did. Since it was very obvious that I wasn't enjoying myself on the ice, how could I expect the audience to enjoy watching me? They were picking up on my discomfort and were feeling it themselves.

As the tour wore on, I withdrew into myself and was afraid to talk to people. It got so bad that I couldn't even look at myself in the mirror. By the time the production was over, and I was in rehearsals for "Skate the Nation," I was lower than low. Earlier, my agent had suggested I talk to a psychiatrist to find out why I was so hard on myself. But I had dismissed the idea. I really didn't think I needed professional help. Now, Nathalie confronted me again. If I didn't do something to change my attitude, she warned, IMG would no longer want to represent me.

I knew Nathalie was serious. But I was having an even more difficult time with this tour because I wasn't the headline female skater. Jennifer Robinson was coming on the tour and would be introduced as the Canadian Champion. Furthermore, Elizabeth Manley was also going to be skating, and of course, Liz is an Olympic silver medallist. I felt like I had been knocked back to third in the spotlight, and I wasn't used to it.

Seeing Jennifer on tour every day was also awkward. I like Jennifer, and as a matter of fact, I am currently helping her with some of her jumps, since we both train in Barrie. I want to see her do well at future international competitions. But in 1996, having her on tour reminded me of what had happened at Nationals, and it was something that I wanted to forget.

I realized, however, that I had to get my act together. I resolved to seek professional help when I arrived home from tour, and in the meanwhile, I would go back to the basics with my skating. Rather than focusing on myself and what I was feeling, I concentrated on each and every move I made on the ice. I tried to avoid thinking about the overall look and what people thought about me, and instead centred on each jump and spin as it happened. And although I was extremely nervous before the first show, I believe I put on a fairly good performance.

I also stopped thinking about myself so much. Liz was having a difficult time executing her double Axel, which was unusual for her because she has one of the best. As I watched her in practice one day, I almost envied her. No matter how much of a hard time she was having, she kept a smile on her face. I had no trouble performing my jumps in practice, but I was still sullen and quiet. Liz, however, managed to joke and laugh even though she was struggling so much. Nobody could figure out what her problem was, and I wondered if it might have anything to do with her skates. We both wore GAMS and since I had a new pair with me, I asked Liz if she would like to try them. She put one on, and immediately was able to execute her jumps. It felt good to help Liz, and I think that by assisting her, I was helping myself.

Little by little, my skating began to improve, and by the time the tour was over, I was feeling better. But I realized that I still needed something more. Keeping the promise to myself and Nathalie, I went to see a psychiatrist, who also happened to be Nathalie's sister-in-law.

I have such mixed feelings about that time. On one hand, it makes me laugh to think that I was so wrapped up in myself, I believed my life was over because I lost Nationals. How could I possibly get so depressed over a sport? On the other hand, I could cry when I remember how utterly sad I was. I guess it doesn't matter how we get there. It's what we do about our feelings that matters.

I saw the therapist for about a year and she really did help me, pointing out that I had put too much pressure on myself because of the promise I had made to my dad. When I failed, I believed I was letting him and the rest of my family down. I'm so glad that I took Nathalie's advise to talk to a professional. It was as if she slapped me on the face and woke me up. Inwardly, I had been screaming for help, but at the same time, I was pushing people away. The problem just kept getting deeper and deeper.

Sometimes we get ourselves into a mental dilemma and it can be very difficult to pull ourselves out. As I have discovered, however, the first step towards healing yourself is to admit that you have a problem. Then you must talk about it. If a trusted friend or family member can't help you, then don't hesitate to get counselling from someone who can. Although it took a few sessions for my therapist to root out the problem, when she did, it was like a light went on. Suddenly, everything became very clear to me. And slowly, I began to enjoy my life and my skating again.

I think we put too much importance on ourselves and what we do. We become too serious. Speaking for myself, I was far too involved in skating. I was living for the sport and putting an unbearable pressure on myself. When that pressure was taken away, I began to like myself again.

I also got married. On August 16, 1997, Jean-Michel and I promised to love each other forever. I was very fortunate to have someone who stayed with me during a time when others may have left. For so long, I had defined my life around skating. When I didn't do well, I thought there was nothing else for me because skating was the only thing I believed I was good at. But here was Jean-Michel, who loved me no matter what. The way he felt about me, and I about him, had nothing to do with skating. We liked and loved each other as people. It was as plain and as simple as that.

Planning our wedding and getting married made me realize there was so much more to life than my sport. Now, I wasn't just a skater, but I was also a wife. Then I discovered fashion design and horseback riding. I may not be the greatest fashion designer or horseback rider in the world, but I love doing these activities. It all comes back to balance.

When we fiercely focus on one goal or one aspect of life, we become so involved that we can't see the forest for the trees. We lose our perspective. When I returned to the ice that September, I skated freer than I had in years. When you're not skating well, it's like you're on an outdoor pond that is full of little bumps. But now I was able to breathe and glide, and it felt like my blades had wings.

I fought through that depressing time, and I made it to the other side a much happier person. I realized my skating was important to me, but it wasn't everything. It was only my career. If you're having a problem, do what you have to do to solve it. Be strong and fight through it. I did, and I know you can too.

CHAPTER NINE

The Joy of Friendship

What can I say about the importance of friendship? My own friends have been with me through the brightest and the darkest of days. Sharing our secrets, fears, hopes, and dreams, we bring comfort and happiness to one another. Like family, who give unconditional love, they make my world complete.

I didn't make many friends in school because I wasn't there enough to maintain close relationships. After class, when other kids were heading to the shopping malls, I was at the skating rink or away at a competition. When I did have the opportunity to see classmates on the occasional weekend or evening, I didn't feel like I belonged. Their circle had tightened and I wasn't a part of the group. I felt rejected, but I wasn't lonely. I had friends in the neighbourhood that I grew up in, and of course, I had my friends at the rink.

From a young age, I felt closer to fellow skaters than I did to almost anyone else. It began with the people I practiced with every day at my club.

We shared common goals and interests, and I couldn't wait to get to the rink to talk to them about the sport we were all so passionate about. As I became further advanced in skating, many of the people I trained with went on to do something else with their lives. But by this time, I had made friends with other skaters from all over the country.

Meeting at various competitions, many of us bonded as teenagers and couldn't wait to see each other again at future events. We strove towards the same dream, and we became even closer as we shared intense emotional moments. Truly, some of the most exciting times of my life were spent with skaters such as Isabelle Brasseur, Sébastien Britten, Brian Orser, Kris and Kristy Wirtz, Elvis Stojko, and Kurt Browning. It's no wonder that I now count these people among my best friends. There is a camaraderie among us that runs deep. And it's not difficult to figure out why. Over the course of many years, we have worked together, travelled together, eaten together, roomed together, and played together. Some of us dated and a few of us even married each other. Spending so much time with one another formed strong connections that exist to this day. We also understand each other. It takes a lot of hard work and commitment to achieve success in this sport, and we respect what each of us has gone through to come this far.

Probably some of the best times I've had both on and off the ice occurred when Kurt Browning was around. Kurt and I hit it off the first time we met at a student skating exchange, where skaters from one province would travel to another province to train at a different club. I was about 13 years old and Kurt was 17 when we met, and although I couldn't understand a word he said, I was drawn to this personable skater from Alberta.

Whenever Kurt was on the ice, your eye was immediately focused on what he was doing. You just knew you were watching a champion in progress. I particularly admired his jumping ability. And I think the feeling was mutual. I loved showing off what I could do in front of the older skaters. I must have caught Kurt's attention because during a team competition, I was one of the first girls chosen to compete on his side. It was a proud moment for me.

Aside from his skating talent, Kurt was absolutely hilarious. In fact, to this day, no one can make me laugh like Kurt Browning and Scott Hamilton. If I'm planning on spending an evening with one or both of them, I know I'm going to come home with my cheeks aching from laughter. Kurt first displayed his comic side to me at the theatre classes we had to attend. While I was not bashful about jumping in front of the other skaters, I was very shy in the performance seminars. Not so with Kurt. He broke us all up with his antics.

The next time we met was at a national training camp a couple of years later. I had arrived feeling quite grown-up, and instantly fell hard for one of the other skaters. Tall and tanned, with blonde streaks running through his hair, this guy was gorgeous. What I didn't know was that he was also gay. When Kurt and some of the other skaters tried to tell me, I set out to prove them wrong, and flirted shamelessly in an attempt to attract him.

One night, we were all out dancing and I managed to get a kiss from the object of my fantasy. It was quite innocent, as everyone looked on. Kurt couldn't stand it another moment, though, and he did everything in his power to stop what I hoped was a budding romance. But there was no need for Kurt to be so upset. The skater wasn't about to change his sexual orientation because of me, and he soon left the party and went to bed. Kurt could barely contain his joy that I had failed in my mission and spent the rest of the night trying to bolster my spirits. We talked, laughed, and got to know each other better. He also introduced me to one of his favourite pastimes: playing pranks on the other skaters.

The entire group of us were staying in a dormitory and everyone else had gone to bed at around 2:00 a.m. Because we had to be in class at 8:00 the following morning, most of the skaters set their alarms for 7:00. Kurt waited until he was sure everyone was fast asleep. Then he and I snuck into the rooms, reset the clocks for 3:00 a.m., and waited for the fun to begin. It was total confusion when the clocks began ringing all at once, and Kurt and I doubled over in laughter as we watched

146

the tired skaters roll out of bed, astonished that morning had come so quickly. Kurt and I then slipped away to pass the rest of the night in quiet conversation. We also shared a little kiss – my one and only romantic encounter with Kurt.

I didn't sleep at all that night and barely managed to get to my class on time the next morning. As I walked in, the other skaters glared in my direction. I guess they didn't think our joke was so funny. I didn't speak much English at the time, but I knew enough to explain that it was all Kurt's idea.

Actually, I wasn't exactly a novice at playing practical jokes. I think I've always had a little bit of a devil in me, which is probably another reason why Kurt and I get along so well. My mischievous side first emerged when I realized I could drive my younger brother crazy by playing tricks on him. Eric was so quiet and could play by himself for hours. But I got bored if there was nothing going on, and my brother was the perfect target for my jokes. If I couldn't think of anything creative, I'd simply chase him all over the house, smothering him in kisses because I knew how much he hated it. I often wonder how Eric put up with me. But he did, and today we are the best of friends.

My antics didn't stop with my brother. I can recall one of my earlier practical jokes that almost turned disastrous. I was at my first national training camp with two good friends, Chantal and Marie Josée. The three of us got along famously.

Although we were all French Canadian, both girls knew how to speak some English and would translate the seminars for me.

Because I hadn't been to the camp before, I was unaware that the other skaters had a ritual. If anybody's birthday fell during the 10 days we were together, that person was thrown into the showers, fully clothed. Lucky me. My birthday was on the first day of the camp. Unbeknownst to me, Marie Josée was off somewhere to inform the other skaters. Meanwhile, I decided to play a trick on her. I convinced Chantal, who was tiny, to get inside one of the suitcases, explaining that it would be very funny to scare Marie Josée by having her open the case to discover Chantal inside. With some reluctance, Chantal crouched down and allowed me to zip up the bag. Assuring my friend that I wouldn't be long, I set off to find Marie Josée. But as soon as I closed the door, which locked behind me, I realized I had dropped the key and it was somewhere on the other side of the door.

I could have told a team leader, or anyone else in charge. That would have been the mature thing to do. But I was 13 years old, and worried that I'd be thrown out of camp if my prank was discovered. Not wanting to alarm Chantal, I decided to say nothing, and ran off to find Marie Josée. She would know what to do.

Spotting my girlfriend in a group of skaters, I opened my mouth to tell her what happened. But before I could get a word out, I was suddenly picked up, carried into the showers, and tossed in. Dripping wet, I eventually made it back to the room with Marie Josée, where we heard Chantal frantically yelling for us to get her out. Peeking under the door, I saw the key laying on the other side, and retrieved it with a coat hanger. Chantal quickly recovered, but she didn't speak to me for a day.

Skaters play jokes on each other all the time. It doesn't matter if we are 13 or 30. The most pranks occur while we're on the road and are trying to cope with the boredom. A couple of years ago, during the last show of the "Skate the Nation" tour, a good one was pulled on Stephen Cousins, who usually keeps us laughing with his comical stories. He was doing a number in which he stood on the ice in his boxer shorts, supposedly drinking vodka. At every other performance, his glass was filled with water. But not on this night. Some of the other skaters had poured out the water and refilled it with liquor. The look on Stephen's face was priceless as he sputtered down the drink in front of an unsuspecting audience.

Aside from enjoying a good laugh, another trait most skaters have in common is a willingness to help each other through rough times. We're not always at our peak in skating, and sometimes landing even the simplest of jumps can be difficult. On one day we feel like we can move mountains, and on another, everything we do can be a challenge. When Scott Hamilton returned to the ice after his victory over cancer, he was having a hard time landing his triple Lutz. Scott must have successfully executed this jump thousands of times over the course of his career, but now he couldn't seem to find his feet. We were all there to help him with his technique, as he tried to get the feeling of the jump back. Nobody was shy about giving whatever assistance they could to this great skater, who we all looked up to. And Scott was grateful that we offered. It's just what we do for each other.

When Kurt and I are on tour together, we are constantly helping each other out with skating technique. For example, if he is having trouble with one of his jumps, I may ask him why he is putting so much energy into it, or point out that he is over-rotating. If I'm having a hard time, he may come to my side and tell me that I'm skating too fast going into the jump. Since we can't see ourselves on the ice, we may not realize what we are doing wrong. Whatever the problem, we're there to help and watch out for each other. If either of our coaches is unable to make it to a competition, we'll take on that role too, and offer moral support from the boards.

Skaters are also fantastic at motivating each other, especially if we're friends. I can recall one World team competition, where my own team needed all the encouragement they could get. Because I was skating particularly well during this time, I was extremely up for the competition. But as for the rest of the team – Isabelle, Lloyd, and Kurt – well, I had never seen such an unmo-

tivated group in my life! Kurt was having difficulties with one of his blades and nothing seemed
to be working for him on the ice. Meanwhile,
Lloyd and Isabelle were having trouble with a
throw and were very frustrated.

The night before the competition, the four of
us had dinner together and my fellow teammates
were so negative, I couldn't believe it. I thought
we had the best team in the event. Lloyd and
Isabelle were famous for exciting the crowd with
their dangerous moves, while Kurt was probably
the best male skater in the world. In my mind,
we couldn't lose. So I became the team cheer-
leader. I said everything positive I could think of,
anything to get them back into a competitive and
winning mode. And I didn't let up. By the time of
the competition, I think the three of them were
sick of my cheery face and words. But it worked.
Our team won!

My friends have all done the same for me at
one time or another. Isabelle and I roomed together throughout most of our amateur years, and
we were as close as sisters. She often gave me
pep talks when I needed some extra motivation.
And she always made me laugh, which helped to
put whatever I was going through in perspective.

When I returned to amateur competition for
the 1996 season, I wondered who my new room-
mate would be for Nationals. I was so used to
Isabelle, who had retired after the Olympics. But
I was fortunate to be paired up with Cathy
Belanger, another skater from Quebec. After I lost

the Canadian Championships and the chance to compete at Worlds, I don't know what I would have done without Cathy. We were supposed to attend a banquet and gala, but I was so stunned and sad from what had happened that I just sat on the bed, unable to move. Cathy didn't say much. She knew it wasn't a time for talk. But she laid out my clothes and shoes and helped me to get dressed. I did whatever she told me to do because I just couldn't think for myself.

I also recall the time when I won my first Nationals, and how my fellow skaters helped me to sort out the mixed feelings I had afterwards. Although I was obviously excited to win, I was having trouble accepting my newfound fame and the big expectations people now had of me. I had never skated for the glory and recognition, and I was overwhelmed by the sudden attention. I had also just signed with IMG and found some of the agents to be intimidating. It wasn't their fault – I was still quite naive and wasn't used to dealing with business people. Because we had the same agents, Kurt often acted as a go-between. I would express my concerns to him, and he in turn would talk to the agents. Through long conversations, Kurt also made me realize how fortunate I was to have won the title. He reminded me that success in anything can be short-lived and that I should learn to enjoy it while it lasted.

Brian Orser also helped me to become more comfortable in my new role as a Canadian Champion. He is one of those rare people who, despite what he is going through himself, will stop and offer words of kindness to others. And he has been through so much. I only hope that I have been as good a friend to him as he has been to me.

I don't think you realize until you get older just how precious friends are. In my youth, I was quick to make judgments and I occasionally held grudges. If someone had hurt my feelings or I felt he or she had broken my trust, I may not have asked for an explanation – and consequently, I may have allowed the person to slip out of my life.

Quite some time ago, I trained with a talented singles skater named Martin Marceau. I was 12 when we met, and although we didn't have the same coach, we trained during the same hours at the rink. We quickly became good friends and our relationship grew deeper over the years. By the time I was 18, we were like brother and sister. One night, just before Martin was going away on tour, he spent the evening with Jean-Michel and me. I later heard that he made a comment about me, and I was furious over the remark. Sadly, I shut this good friend out of my life.

Many years passed, and although our paths crossed now and then, we never shared the closeness we once had. Then, a few months ago, I received a phone call. It was Marie Josée, who asked me if I was sitting down. My stomach immediately lurched as I realized I was about to get bad news. She told me that Martin had been diagnosed with cancer, and that it was very serious. She also said that he wanted to speak with me and left his telephone number.

I was so shaken that it took 24 hours for me to calm down enough to call him. But when I did, it was so good to hear his voice. We both cried. A short time later, Martin and I got together and talked about what had happened. I couldn't even tell him what I was angry at because I honestly didn't remember. I so regretted the time we wasted. Martin is doing much better now, and he may have actually won out over this terrible disease. I can only pray, because I don't want to lose him again.

My friends are my lifelines during troubling times. They keep me balanced and grounded. I don't know why, but it's hard to make good friends as we get older. Maybe we begin to trust people a little less, or maybe we think we don't have the time to establish close relationships. So we must nurture the friendships we have. They are like gifts to be cherished and I couldn't imagine my life without them.

CHAPTER TEN

Never Give Up!

At the end of the 1996 season, I came very close to giving up skating. It would have been so easy to run away from the pain and disappointment. But it also would have been the biggest mistake of my life. I would have been leaving something that I had a heartfelt passion for, and I'm sure it would have left me feeling empty inside. I also don't believe that the poor image I had of myself would have ever fully healed. By sticking it out, I emerged more confident with the realization that I have the strength to face whatever challenges may be thrown my way.

As I worked through my sadness, I noticed that skating became so much easier. And the more I performed in this new frame of mind, the more fun I had on the ice. I felt lighter and more care-free than I had in years. And I began to embrace the sport again, appreciating each and every moment I spent entertaining an audience. It was as if I had rediscovered myself.

I'm thriving as a professional skater and am so grateful for the life this profession has given me. I've met people from movie stars to heads of state and travelled to places that, at one time, I could only fantasize about. I've toured with the best skaters in the business, and done commercials, talk shows, and television specials. I even skated with Tara Lipinski in the film "Ice Angels." You would think I'd be used to this lifestyle by now, but every now and then I have to pinch myself to make sure I'm not dreaming. There are countless stories I could tell you about experiences I've had that have come as a direct result of what I do for a living. But let me share a few of my more memorable moments – like the time I met the Prime Minister of Canada, under truly bizarre circumstances.

I'd been to many banquets and dinners before, during which I'd been introduced to various dignitaries and other important people. You go through a receiving line, shake hands, say a few words, and move on. But the night I met Jean Chrétien wasn't like this at all. Indeed, it was one of the strangest nights of my life.

I was appearing at an event in Ottawa called "Winterlude." We were supposed to be skating on the Rideau Canal, but it had rained the week before. The ice on the river had melted and frozen over again, and was totally unsuitable for a show. Instead, we performed on an outdoor rink behind the Governor General's residence. After the show, I was driving around the city, sightseeing with Jean-Michel, one of the sponsors of the show, and the fellow who organized "Winterlude." Having already seen some of the more interesting places in the capital, we decided to drive by the Prime Minister's house, which was surrounded by high walls. The gates were open, however, and before I could utter a single word of protest, we drove in.

I was as curious as everyone else to see the house, but I was very nervous that we may be doing something that wasn't permitted. I was right. Within 15 seconds, our car was surrounded by several burly men with guns who demanded we explain our presence. In a small voice, one of the guys we were with told the security guard that I was in town performing and had wanted to see where the Prime Minister lived. As he spoke, I shrunk as low as I could in the seat, wishing I was anywhere but there. Then someone else approached, who had emerged from one of the five limousines parked in the driveway. He too had a gun. By now, I was more than worried. And I could have kicked Jean-Michel, who couldn't control a fit of the giggles. As usual, he was seeing the funny side.

The second man told us to wait, and I began to tremble as I imagined myself being led away in handcuffs. I was in such an anxious state that I was totally unprepared for what he said upon his return. The guard told us that although the Prime Minister was just about to meet the new Governor General's train, he would be delighted to meet with us for a few minutes!

Now picture this. I was in a heavy winter coat, pants, boots, and earmuffs. My hair was a mess and I hadn't checked my makeup in hours. And I was about to meet the Prime Minister of our country. I couldn't believe this was happening. Standing at the front door – formally dressed, I might add – Mr. Chrétien and his wife asked us in. They were so casual about our appearance that you would have thought they were expecting us. Worrying that I would leave puddles of melted snow on the expensive carpets and highly polished wood floors, I began to remove my boots, but Mrs. Chrétien told me to leave them on. Then our unlikely group was taken for a tour of the entire house, which ended in the Prime Minister's office. In the very room where he was televised addressing the nation, he wrote notes to both Jean-Michel and myself, thanking us for being such good ambassadors to the country. Amazing!

I don't follow politics too closely, and wouldn't want to give an opinion on parties or their policies. But if anyone asked, I'd be the first to say that our Prime Minister is one of the most friendly and charming individuals I have ever met.

There must be something about me that draws celebrities to my side when I don't look my best. One year, I was in Toronto shooting a segment for television that was going to be shown during the Olympics. We heard that Céline Dion was performing for a corporate group next door to our set, and because I was skating to one of her songs, my producer thought it would be terrific publicity to get some shots of her and me together. I honestly didn't believe she would be available on such short notice, and didn't think much else about it. But an hour or so later, she strolled into the room, looking like the diva she is. Tall, slender, and elegantly dressed, the singer towered over me in the highest of heels. Needless to say, I didn't feel at all glamourous compared to her. If only I had been wearing my skates, which added a couple of inches to my height, and one of my pretty skating outfits. But no. I was in running shoes and a bulky purple and white track suit.

Céline was obliging and gracious, and patiently posed with me for the camera. She was also a little mischievous, which I didn't realize until the photographs were developed and sent to me much later. In one, the famous songstress had put two fingers behind my head in the "V" sign. So much for decorum.

While we're on the subject of meeting celebrities in unusual ways, I have to tell you how I met Curtis Joseph, the goaltender for the Toronto Maple Leafs. I have been introduced to many hockey players over the years, but never like this. Just before Jean-Michel and I got married, we were racking our brains trying to think of memorable gifts for our attendants. Since our ring bearer was goaltender on his team, and was also a huge fan of the Maple Leafs' goalie, Jean-Michel wanted to present him with an autographed hockey stick. We knew Curtis had recently moved into our neighbourhood, but neither of us had ever met him. One day, Jean-Michel asked me to accompany him to the Joseph household, where he would try to muster the courage to ask for a hockey stick.

"No way," I told my husband-to-be. I often had children coming to my door asking for autographs, or ringing my bell only to scamper away as I answered. But they were children and could be excused for the intrusions they sometimes caused. To have an adult knock on my door with the same request was a different matter. I don't mind giving my autograph to anyone. I've even asked for a few myself over the years, but there is a proper time and place. The thought of knocking on Curtis Joseph's door for such a request made me cringe in embarrassment. But Jean-Michel wanted that stick, and he didn't want to go alone.

I don't know how he talked me into it, but a short time later the two of us were standing in front of the famed goaltender's house. As we tried to decide how we were going to ask for the favour, Curtis came walking out of his garage. Fortunately, he recognized me and didn't chase us off the property. After we explained why we were there, he turned around, went back into the garage, and returned with an autographed stick. What a nice man!

Over the course of my career, I've met many other interesting and well-known people, from Bryan Adams, who came to a show to take pictures of some of the female skaters (Bryan is also a photographer and was putting a book together to benefit breast cancer research), to singing sensation Christina Aguilera, who I happened upon at a car race in the United States. That's the fun part of my job. But fascinating people aside, let me assure you that the life of a professional skater is not all glamour and glitter.

Take touring, for example. For someone like me, who loves to travel, being on the road can be a wonderful experience. But it can also be very tedious. We spend long hours on buses and airplanes and do whatever we can to relieve the boredom. Some of the skaters play cards, watch movies, or catch up on their correspondence with their laptops. Others take advantage of the travelling time by getting some sleep they may have missed the night before. As for me, I like to talk with my friends while doing needlework. Once we reach our destination, we check into a hotel and usually make plans to meet for a quiet dinner. There is little or no partying before a show because we need to conserve our energy for the upcoming performance. Instead, we eat, work out, and try to get to bed at a half-decent hour. The next morning, we're up early and off to the rink, where we practice, play ping-pong, kick around a soccer ball, or do our laundry. I don't mean to put you to sleep here, but that's what life on the road is like.

It isn't all humdrum, however. An hour before the show begins, the backstage area comes alive and you can feel the electricity in the air. As we apply makeup and slip into the most beautiful costumes imaginable, we can hear the stage manager call out how many minutes are left before showtime. At the five-minute mark, we put on our skates and take our places behind the black curtain that separates us from the audience. The lights go down, the spotlights go on, and you can hear the crowd clapping above the music. It's pure magic.

Throughout the show, I am filled with excitement. The adrenalin courses through my body and I experience a high that is hard to describe. There isn't the pressure of competition. It is just me and the audience, and I'm back to being the eight-year-old child who loves to entertain. Afterwards, it's very hard to come down. In most cities, we attend a reception where the skaters sign autographs. Although many of the people are sponsors or other VIPs, there are also fans at the receptions, and I especially enjoy interacting with these people. Then it's back to the hotel, where I usually find it impossible to sleep. Most evenings, I will head downstairs for a glass of wine or a cup of tea. And inevitably, the rest of the cast will appear one by one. Like me, they need to unwind. The next day, we're back on the road doing it all over again.

You may also believe that appearing in television specials or commercials sounds more like play than work. Wrong! There is a huge effort involved in putting these productions together, and everything takes so much time. The lighting, sound, and sets have to be perfect, and if anything is amiss, we can be standing around for hours until it's corrected. The director will tell us to take a five-minute break, but we'll be lucky to start again in an hour. Because our costumes can't have the slightest wrinkle in them when the cameras are ready to roll, sitting or laying down is out of the question. We even have to drink through straws so our makeup doesn't get messed up. I've been on sets at 8:00 a.m. and have still been standing around waiting at 11:00 p.m. The sheer boredom of it all can make you crazy.

• • • • •

In my life as a professional skater, I have competed in a wide array of events. I took every competition I entered very seriously, and put much effort into keeping up my technical skills and preparing unique programs. I didn't win every competition, but I was usually pleased with the results. I was never more proud, however, than when I won the 2000 Canadian Pro-Am Championships. Having come first over some of the best amateur women in the world, I had finally fulfilled a long-standing dream. This competition was my World Championships. I had proven to myself and the rest of the world that I was good enough. It was such a satisfying feeling, and I realized that if I had quit skating in 1996, I would never have known that I could do it.

Although I was busy the following year, it was also a time of reflection for me. Since winning the title was the ultimate peak in my career as a professional skater, I wondered what more I could do and wanted to do in my sport. After much thought, I realized it was time for me to step back a little. I would still skate in special events, television shows, and the occasional competition, but I would stop touring. That meant leaving "Stars on Ice." It was a difficult decision to make, but there was so much more I want to do with my life, and not all of it involved skating. Somewhere, somehow, I had to make the time.

But before I left touring altogether, I wanted to travel the country once more to thank the fans who had supported me through all my ups and downs. And this is why I prepared my farewell tour, which played in most of the major venues across Canada. With a showcase of skaters, including Brian Orser, Elizabeth Manley, Lloyd Eisler and Isabelle Brasseur, Gary Beacom, David Pelletier and Jamie Salé, Jennifer Robinson, Patrice Lauzon and Marie-France Dubreuil, Emanuel Sandhu, Kris and Kristy Wirtz, Jerod Swallow and Elizabeth Punsalan, and Elvis Stojko, it was not only a gathering of great skaters, but a gathering of my friends. The one name missing from my tour was Kurt's, and as much as I would have loved for him to have been with us, my dear friend was already committed to an event of his own at the time.

Organizing this tour and being involved in every aspect of the show were among the most challenging ventures I had ever taken on. From coordinating the skaters, to purchasing the props, to working with choreographers David Wilson and Lori Nickol, I had never done so much running around in my life. I even designed many of the costumes, which was personally rewarding. As you know, fashion design is a career I want to pursue in the future.

Rehearsals for the tour were to start in late September, 2001. Although I was still putting together last-minute details, everything looked like it was coming together nicely. Then the unthinkable happened.

September 11th started out like any other day. I was to meet some of the skaters in Halifax, where we were going to perform in a show for the corporate sponsor. My plane left Toronto at 8:45 a.m. It wasn't until I arrived in Halifax that I learned of the horrific tragedy that had occurred in the United States only a few minutes after my own plane had taken off. Like everyone else, I was shocked, stunned, and frightened.

Only a few of the other skaters were in Halifax, having arrived the night before. Of course, our show was cancelled, and it was just as well. I don't think any of us could have concentrated on skating. That night, I sat in my hotel room trying to finish the costume designs I was working on. It was imperative that I get them done, but I just couldn't focus. I needed to be with my friends at such a heartbreaking time. Leaving the drawings on the table, I joined the other skaters at a restaurant, where we talked for hours.

With no flights scheduled in the immediate future, we decided to drive back to Toronto. And it was on this trip that I wondered if I should cancel or postpone my tour. In the course of a few minutes, our world had changed forever, and suddenly skating and entertainment didn't seem so relevant. When I arrived home, I still hadn't made a decision.

As I continued to watch the events unfold on television, I wanted to help but didn't know how. And then it dawned on me. Instead of sitting at home and doing nothing, I would stage the tour and donate a portion of ticket sales to the relief fund. It may not be much in the grand scheme of things, I thought, but at least it would be something.

• • • • •

Last March, I watched the 2001 World Championships on television, during which an Italian skater named Sylvia Fontana made me sit up and take notice. She hadn't had the best year from a competitive standpoint, and had gone into Worlds even though the people of her country doubted her ability. With a will that only comes from the heart of a champion, Sylvia didn't give up. At Worlds, she skated two incredible programs and came tenth. For the first time in years, Italy had a woman in the top 10. Sylvia positively glowed with joy after her performance, and I knew what she was feeling. It was personal satisfaction.

A few months later, when I was out on tour with "Skate the Nation," I ran into Sylvia and mentioned how inspired I had been by her performance. She looked into my eyes and told me something that gave me the shivers. *I had been her inspiration.* She went on to say that she had watched my performance at the 1991 World Championships, and decided she wanted to be like me. There, I had skated to Italian music, never dreaming that I was influencing a young girl with big dreams.

I'm often asked which skater I looked up to in my youth, and it is a difficult question to answer because there wasn't just one person. I admired Elizabeth Manley's speed, Katarina Witt's elegance, Brian Orser's jumps, and Tracey Wilson and Rob McCall's creativity. When I'm skating, my style is a combination of all those people. But there's more to it than that. I admired these great skaters for their ability on the ice, but also for who they were as people. Each and every one had challenges, but none of them gave up. They didn't quit because the going got tough.

That's the true inspiration. And it's what we're all facing now, as individuals and as a world. Don't give up hope, and don't ever give up on your dreams. With determination, focus, and passion, they really can come true. And no one knows this better than me.

Adieu . . . until we meet again.